T0030445

NIVEL
1

Los Trenes

Amy Shields

NATIONAL
GEOGRAPHIC

Washington, D.C.

Que sigan viajando mucho los trenes Silver Star, Empire, Vermonter y Adirondack.

Publicado por National Geographic Partners, LCC. Washington, DC 20036.

Derechos de autor © 2011 National Geographic Society.
Derechos de autor de la traducción © 2024 National Geographic Partners, LLC.

Todos los derechos reservados. La reproducción parcial o total del material sin el permiso escrito de la editorial está prohibida.

NATIONAL GEOGRAPHIC y Yellow Border Design son marcas registradas de National Geographic Society, usadas bajo licencia.

Diseñado por Lauren Sciortino and Gustavo Tello

Créditos fotográficos

Tapa, All Canada Photos/Alamy; 1, Steve Criso; 3, Mr. Klein/Shutterstock; 4 (arriba, derecha), Jean Brooks/robertharding/Getty Images; 4 (abajo, deracha), Arvind Garg; 4 (centro, izquierda), Scott Barrow/Getty Images; 5 (centro, izquierda), Steve Eshom; 5 (arriba, izquierda), Benjamin Rondel/Getty Images; 5 (arriba, derecha), Claver Carroll/Getty Images; 5 (abajo), Kevin Fleming/Corbis/VCG/Getty Images; 6-7, Glow Images/Getty Images; 7 (abajo), Rebecca Hale, National Geographic Staff; 8-9, Nigel Hicks/Dorling Kindersley/Getty Images; 9 (recuadro), Larry Dale Gordon/Photographer's Choice/Getty Images; 10 (arriba), Richard T. Nowitz/Getty Images; 10 (abajo), Rebecca Hale, National Geographic Staff; 11 (arriba), altrendo travel/Stockbyte/Getty Images; 11 (abajo), Chris Harris/Getty Images; 12, Bettmann/Getty Images; 13, Corbis Historical/Getty Images; 14, Rebecca Hale, National Geographic Staff; 15 (arriba), H. Armstrong Roberts/Retrofile/Getty Images; 15 (abajo), Bettmann/Getty Images; 16 (arriba), Lee Prince/Shutterstock; 16 (abajo), Ajit Kumar/Shutterstock; 16 (centro), Diana Walters/iStockphoto.com; 17 (arriba), Martin Ruetschi; 17 (abajo), Justin Horrocks/iStockphoto.com; 17 (centro), National Postal Museum/Smithsonian Institution; 18-19, Kent Kobersteen/National Geographic Image Collection; 19 (recuadro), James Lauritz/Digital Vision/Getty Images; 20, ClassicStock/Alamy Stock Photo; 20 (recuadro), Rebecca Hale, National Geographic Staff; 21 (arriba), H. Armstrong Roberts/Classicstock; 21 (abajo), Bettmann/Getty Images; 22, Rebecca Hale, National Geographic Staff; 23, courtesy Royale Indian Rail Tours Ltd.; 24-25, Greg Dale/National Geographic Image Collection; 26-27, Bryan F. Peterson; 27 (derecha), Rebecca Hale, National Geographic Staff; 28, Rebecca Hale, National Geographic Staff; 29, Paul Miller/Bloomberg via Getty Images; 30, Kazumasa Yanai/Getty Images; 31, mountainberryphoto/iStockphoto.com; 31 (recuadro), Rebecca Hale, National Geographic Staff; 32 (arriba, izquierda), Rebecca Hale, National Geographic Staff; 32 (arriba, derecha), H. Armstrong Roberts/Retrofile/Getty Images; 32 (abajo, izquierda), Bryan F. Peterson; 32 (abajo, derecha), Kent Kobersteen/National Geographic Collection

Libro en rústica ISBN:
978-1-4263-7651-1
Encuadernación de biblioteca reforzada ISBN:
978-1-4263-7664-1

Impreso en los Estados Unidos de América
23/WOR/1

Tabla de contenidos

Muchos trenes

Tren de vapor, tren de carga, tren de circo, tren de frío.

Tren de granos,
tren de carbón,
tren de pasajeros.

¡Todos abordo!

¿Has viajado en un tren de vapor? ¿Has escuchado el traqueteo de las ruedas sobre la vía? ¿Has escuchado el sonido *wuuuu-wuu* de su silbato? ¿Sonó la campana *ring-ring-ring* en el cruce del tren?

VOCABULARIO

MAQUINISTA: Una persona que conduce el tren

Me llamo Gary y este es mi tren. Yo soy el maquinista.

A todo vapor

Los trenes de vapor llevan piezas móviles ruidosas.

El calor por quemar carbón o petróleo convierte al agua en vapor. El vapor mueve los pistones.

Los pistones mueven las bielas. Las bielas hacen girar las ruedas y mueven al tren por las vías.

biela

Los trenes tienen ruedas especiales para las vías. La mayoría de las vías tienen rieles de acero y durmientes de madera o concreto. Los rieles se clavan a los durmientes.

rieles de acero

Los autos no pueden ir por los rieles.

durmientes de concreto

Los trenes recorren vías sobre valles.

Circulan sobre vías a través de montañas.

Un nuevo Estados Unidos

Irlandeses y chinos ayudaron a construir las vías del tren hace unos 150 años. Fueron los nuevos estadounidenses.

Cuando terminaron las vías, estas se extendían por todo el país. Se mudó más gente al oeste. Se crearon ciudades a lo largo de las vías. Se construyeron bancos y tiendas. Los trenes les traían dinero y oro.

Los asaltantes querían robar el oro y el dinero. Butch Cassidy y el Sundance Kid fueron asaltantes. Robaban trenes con su banda criminal. Después huían en sus caballos. Se repartían el botín en su escondite, el cuchitril.

Asaltantes retuvieron a muchos trenes.

VOCABULARIO

BOTÍN: Oro y dinero robados

15

6 MARAVILLAS
de los trenes

1 Algunos trenes bala **flotan** magnéticamente **sobre los rieles.**

Muchas estaciones de tren se llaman **Union Station.** Las utilizan **diferentes** líneas de **trenes.**

2

El **Reina de las Hadas** de **India** es **uno** de los **trenes** de vapor **más antiguos.**

3

16

4

El **túnel de tren más largo del mundo** mide **56 km** de **largo.** Atraviesa las montañas de los Alpes. Se inauguró en **2017.**

En 1888, **hallaron un cachorro** en el **vagón de correos.** Lo llamaron **Owney.** Iba en los trenes de correos y se volvió su **amuleto de la suerte.**

5

6

En inglés, **"railfan"** es **una persona** a la **que le gustan los trenes.** Suelen irse de vacaciones **en trenes.**

Trucos de los trenes

VOCABULARIO

PLATAFORMA GIRATORIA: Pieza de vía de tren que se puede girar

¿Qué sucede cuando un tren llega al final de la vía? Algunas vías ferroviarias llegan hasta una plataforma giratoria. La locomotora se pone sobre la plataforma. *Runrúúúún.* La plataforma gira. La locomotora sale en una nueva dirección.

La plataforma giratoria es un gran invento para los trenes. Aquí hay unos más.

Mira algunos de estos inventos.

vagón tirado por mula

La gente pensó en formas de viajar por las vías incluso sin trenes.

dresina

Trenes de pasajeros

La gente va en tren al trabajo. También lo toman para ir de vacaciones.

Ahora hay vías de tren por todo el mundo.

El Maharajas' Express es un tren de la India. Lo llaman un palacio sobre ruedas.

Se construyó para la realeza. La gente se va de vacaciones en este tren. Es un viaje agradable y lento por el país.

¿Quieres ir más rápido? Los trenes bala son rápidos como balas. Viajan a más de 442 kilómetros por hora. Se mueven sobre las vías de tren.

Algunos son impulsados por locomotoras. Otros tienen motores para
cada vagón. Los trenes bala son de
pasajeros, para personas.

Los trenes bala son eléctricos.
Llevan pantógrafos encima de
algunos vagones.

La electricidad viene del carbón, el mismo que impulsa los motores de vapor.

Los cables en lo alto pasan electricidad a los pantógrafos.

pantógrafo

VOCABULARIO

PANTÓGRAFO: Brazos de metal en el techo de un tren que atrapan electricidad de los cables

27

Trenes de carga

Los trenes de carga llevan cosas como zapatillas y celulares. Los trenes de carga más largos miden 3.2 kilómetros. Tienen locomotoras de diésel. Las que van adelante tiran de los vagones. Las que van atrás, empujan.

La mayoría de los artículos que hay en tu casa viajó en un tren alguna vez.

locomotora diésel

Cuando pasa un tren, los ferroviarios se paran a observar. La próxima vez que veas uno pasar, saluda con la mano al poderoso tren traqueteando por la vía.

GLOSARIO

BOTÍN: Oro y dinero robados

MAQUINISTA: Una persona que conduce el tren

PANTÓGRAFO: Brazos de metal en el techo de un tren que atrapan electricidad de los cables

PLATAFORMA GIRATORIA: Pieza de vía de tren que se puede girar

top, and reach for the clasps at my neck. My fingers are like
usages now, swelling and splitting, but somehow I manage to
nble one clasp open, then the other. My helmet flies away, and
rd vacuum sucks everything out of me.

Air.

Blood.

Shit.

Everything.

I should be dead now, but I'm not, and I can't understand why.
I open my cracked mouth and pull in a lungful of nothing. Be-
re I can use it to scream, though, I snap awake, wide-eyed and
eating in the coal-black dark.

it on the floor, sit down on the bed and start unlacing my boots.
Eight sits down next to me.

"Anyway," he says, "what's going on out there? The feed just
says four accidental deaths and one gone missing, all outside the
dome. How does that happen?"

I finish with the boots, pull them off, and lie back on the bed.
"Well," I say. "First, they weren't all outside, strictly speaking.
One was in the main lock, which by the way is no longer in ser-
vice, since they just used the murder hole."

That hangs in the air for a long, awkward moment.

"The murder hole," Eight says finally. "They used it on what?"

I fold my hands behind my head and close my eyes. "Creepers."

Eight laughs, with a little more warmth this time. "Okay. Got
it. You're shitting me. Really, what happened?"

"Really, they vented plasma into the lock to kill creepers that
had breached the decking, and roasted a mostly dead Security
goon named Gallaher in the process."

"Creepers are animals, Seven. You don't use live plasma to kill
an animal."

"I don't think you're hearing me," I say. "*They breached the
deck.*"

"By 'breached' you mean . . ."

"I mean they cut directly through the decking and started peeling it away."

"Peeling it away? You mean they . . . took it?"

I shrug. "Seems like it. This planet is metal-poor, you know.
Maybe they need it for something."

"Huh." He scratches the top of his head. "Scoot over."

I slide over to make room for him, and he lies down next to
me. This still feels weird, but there's been so much weirdness in
my life in the past twenty-four hours that it barely registers.

"It's not like anybody thought they were harmless," Eight

says, "but it's a little hard to swallow an animal being able to rip through the ship's decking, isn't it?"

"You're not wrong." I'm about to go on, but I have to stop to yawn. I haven't slept except in two-hour stretches since the night before last. "I didn't see the bit with the decking, to be honest, but I saw the hole in the floor of the main lock. I also saw a bunch of creepers take down two fully armored goons and one very frightened biologist. It was not pretty."

"You're saying you saw creepers bite through ten-mil fiber armor?"

"Well," I say, "not that specifically. I saw them crawling around on ten-mil fiber armor, and I saw the guys wearing the armor go down. The actual biting-through-armor part was pretty strongly implied, though."

Eight rises up on one elbow and leans over me. "That doesn't make sense. Species don't evolve abilities that don't have uses in their environment. Why would an ice worm evolve the ability to bite through armor designed to stop a ten-gram LA slug?"

"That's an excellent question," I say, and yawn again. "I will definitely give you a good answer for it when I wake up."

Eight keeps talking, but his words slur into a dull background hum. The last conscious thing I remember is the bed shifting slightly as he stands.

ALMOST EVERY NIGHT for the past few weeks, I've had the same recurring . . . dream? No, more like a vision, I guess. It always comes just when I'm drifting off, or just when I'm waking. This is one reason why I haven't been uploading. I'm a little concerned that I might have suffered some kind of glitch during the regen process. If I did, I don't want to inject any of it into my personality record.

More importantly, I don't want anyone in psych to notice, and suggest that maybe they ought to scrap me and try again.

In the dream I'm back on Midgard, out in the woods along the crest of the Ullr Mountains. There's a trail the hundred kilometers of untouched wilderness filled with falls, hundred-kilometer vistas, and trees that have been g since the original terraformers seeded the place three h years ago. I've walked it end-to-end four times. There's a empty space on Midgard, but those mountains are the em place on a mostly empty planet. In all the time I spent out t I don't think I saw more than two or three other human bei

I'm camped for the night, sitting on a log in front of a l fire, staring into the flames. So far, so good, right? Maybe just homesick. But then I hear a noise, like someone clearing throat. I look up, and there's this giant caterpillar sitting acro the fire from me.

I know I should be freaking out right now, but I'm not. That the part of the whole experience that's most like an actual dream

The caterpillar and I talk—or try to, anyway. His mou moves, and sounds come out that sound like words, but I ca make any sense of them. I tell him to stop, to slow down, th if he would just speak a little more clearly I could understa what he's saying. He doesn't, though. He just keeps going, u the listening makes my head start to ache. I look into the fire running backward, unburning the pile of sticks it's feedin and sucking smoke back out of the air. When I look up again caterpillar is fading, becoming less and less substantial, until the smile remains.

Eventually even the smile disappears, and as it does I slid this half world into a real dream, one I've had on and years. I'm Mickey2, out on the hull of the *Drakkar* again, ing back toward the forward lock as my skin sloughs aw my blood begins seeping from ruptured vessels, covering fever sweat and draining into my mouth, my throat, m

MICKEY2 WAS MY shortest-lived instantiation.

Mickey3 was my longest.

It took me a while to get over what happened to One. You never forget your first kiss, right? Well, you never forget your first death either, and the death that my original body experienced was a pretty traumatic one. Two's ending shouldn't have been as scarring, mostly because I didn't actually remember anything about being him—but just knowing that what he went through was bad enough that explosive decompression seemed like a good idea weighed on me. I spent most of my time those first few weeks as Three moping around, jumping at every loud noise and waiting for something bad to happen.

Time went by, though. Weeks turned to months, months turned to the better part of a year full of nothing, and nothing bad happened. Funny thing. As it turns out, even waiting expectantly for a sudden, violent death gets boring after a while.

It was about that time that my general interest in history morphed into a morbid interest in the histories of failed colonies. You wouldn't think they'd have that sort of material available in the ship's library—bad for morale and all—but they did. My teachers didn't talk about the failures in school. I wouldn't necessarily call what they fed us *propaganda*, but in every subject, from biology to history to physics, they made sure to weave in something about the importance and nobility of the Diaspora, and the idea that it's been an uninterrupted parade of successes as humanity has spread across the spiral arm was pretty strongly implied if never actually stated—so I was surprised to learn that there have been almost as many failed efforts as successes over the past thousand years.

When colonists set out in a ship like the *Drakkar*, they really have no idea what they're likely to find at the end of the journey. The physics of antimatter drives dictate that they only work at scale, and antimatter production is insanely difficult and expensive, so a world looking to launch a colony ship can't just send out probes to a bunch of likely stars to scout things out before they go. So, they make do with what they can observe from their home system. When we left Midgard, for example, we knew we were headed to a G-type main-sequence star. We knew it had at least three smallish, rocky planets, and that one of them was at the outer edge of the star's Goldilocks zone. We knew that planet—our target—had water vapor and at least some free oxygen in its atmosphere, from which we inferred that it almost certainly supported some form of life.

That was about it, honestly—and because Midgard and Niflheim aren't actually that far apart as these things go, and also because our powers of observation have improved substantially as time has gone on, we knew more than a lot of colony ships have. One of the shortest records I found was for an expedition launched from Asher's World a bit more than a hundred years ago. Asher's World is about as far out toward the rim as we've ventured, and the stars are spread thin there. Their target was over twenty lights distant, which is at the outer range of what a colony ship can do, and maybe a little beyond. The adult colonists were old, and tired, and really hungry by the time they finished their deceleration burn, and their ship was practically falling apart.

Unfortunately, the world they'd been targeting wasn't in the orbit they'd been expecting. It was just slightly too close to its star. They'd been fooled by the fact that they'd seen O_2 absorption spectra in its atmosphere. There was some oxygen there, but there was no liquid water, because the surface temperature was too high to permit it. Theory said that shouldn't have been possible, but the universe is a funny place, and it was what it was. Their best guess was that the planet may have been habitable—may in fact have been inhabited by something or other that was able to split carbon from CO_2 and produce free oxygen—but that a runaway greenhouse effect, something like the one that was pushing the limits of habitability of some parts of old Earth in the years before the Diaspora, had fairly recently sterilized the place. If they were right, the residual oxygen they'd detected just hadn't had time to bind itself out of the atmosphere yet.

With a hundred years to terraform, they might have been able to make it work. They didn't have a hundred years, though. With the condition of their ship, they probably didn't have ten. So, they beamed their findings back home, then put their ship into a stable orbit, doped everyone who wanted to be doped, and popped their air locks. As Two could tell you, explosive decompression isn't a fun time, but at least it's quick.

Reading that got me thinking about Two. That sent me into a spiral that lasted the better part of a month.

The thing that pulled me back out of that spiral was Nasha.

I'd seen Nasha around, obviously, going all the way back to Himmel Station. When you're living in a giant canister with fewer than two hundred other people, you see everybody around at some point. I'd never spoken to her, though—mostly for the same reason I'd never spoken to most of the other people on the

Drakkar. Lots of them didn't want anything to do with me, and I compensated by not wanting anything to do with them.

We met for real about a year after the collision that wound up killing One and Two. We were well into the coast phase of the journey by then, humming along through the vacuum at just a hair under point-nine *c,* weightless and on short rations and bored out of our minds. Command had ordered all personnel to spend at least two hours of every duty cycle in the carousel—nominally so that we'd still have bones and whatnot when we finally made landfall, but actually I think so that we'd be less likely to start murdering one another just to break up the monotony.

The carousel was exactly what it sounds like: a spinning ring around the waist of the ship a hundred and twenty meters across, with a flat, rubberized inner surface about six meters wide. They had it going at three revs per minute, which was fast enough to get us about half a standard g, but also slow enough that you could stand upright without having the Coriolis effect bring up your lunch.

We were supposed to spend our time in the carousel working out, but as long as we were in there for the designated time, nobody who mattered really seemed to care what we did. There were a few prigs who'd shoot you a look as they ran past if you weren't doing squat thrusts or yoga or practicing Krav Maga, but as far as I know none of them ever actually went to the trouble of filing a delinquency report on anyone.

I'd been pretty good about jogging around the ring at least a few times every day, right up until One and Two went down. After that, though, my motivation dropped off pretty radically. Not much point in worrying about bone mineral density and muscle tone when your bones and muscles have the shelf life of an open package of yogurt, right? I started bringing a tablet to the carousel, finding a place as far away from the squat thrusters as I could to plant myself against a wall, and reading through the records of other beachhead colonies. That's when I learned all about Asher's World, and Roanoke, and a bunch of other recent disasters.

Needless to say, reading that kind of stuff didn't increase my motivation to exercise.

So one day I was there in the carousel, squatting against the wall and reading through a first-person account of a near-failure that had occurred almost a thousand years prior, on what's now one of the most heavily populated worlds in the Union. The issue there was persistent agricultural failure, which they eventually traced to a virus that was endemic in the soil. They didn't have bio-cyclers then, and the narrator made it sound like things got pretty hungry before they cracked the problem.

I was just getting to the part where the head of the colony's Biology Section, who also happens to be the narrator, heroically saves the day with a tailored phage that clears the way for human-friendly plants to grow—while coincidentally wiping out the microorganism that had made it possible for local plants to grow, and thereby completely destroying the native ecosystem—when a boot nudged my shoulder, hard enough to knock me half over. I looked up to see a woman in black Security togs standing over me, arms folded across her chest.

"Hey," she said. "Shouldn't you be doing push-ups right now?"

I glared up at her. She broke into a grin and squatted down beside me.

"I'm just messing with you. You're the Expendable, right?"

"I'm Mickey Barnes," I said. "Who are you?"

"Mickey Barnes, huh? Don't you mean Mickey3 now?"

Ouch.

"Yeah," I said. "That."

She settled back against the wall. I sighed, straightened up, and tucked my tablet into my chest pocket.

"I'm Nasha Adjaya," she said. "Combat pilot."

I glanced over at her. Her braids had fallen across her face, but I could still see the grin.

"Combat pilot, huh? You must be pals with Berto."

"Gomez? Yeah, he's okay. Better pog-ball player than a pilot, but we get along."

I smiled. "You're not wrong. I wonder which we'll need more of when we get where we're going."

She leaned toward me. "You're not questioning the importance of combat pilots to the mission, are you?"

"Yeah," I said. "Kind of. Do they need a lot of those on beachhead colonies? I mean, do we expect to make landfall on a planet that's already got an air force?"

Her grin widened. "Guess you never know, right? Just 'cause it's never happened before doesn't mean it never will."

"There's only two of you," I said. "Better hope it's a *small* air force, right?"

She laughed. "Doesn't matter, friend. I'm a hell of a pilot."

"Yeah," I said. "I'm sure that's true."

We sat in silence then. I was starting to wonder whether I should pull my tablet back out, or maybe just get up and leave, when she turned to look at me. I looked back. The grin was gone and her eyes had narrowed. Her irises were so dark they were almost black.

"So," she said. "What's dying like?"

I shrugged. "Like being born, only backward."

"Ha! I like that." She smiled. "You know, you're pretty cute for a zombie."

"Thanks," I said. "I use a lot of moisturizer."

She touched my hand, then ran one finger up along my forearm. "I bet you do," she said.

Her smile morphed into a leer.

"I just bet . . . you . . . do."

IT WAS LATER, and we were back in my rack, halfway to naked and tangled around one another in the darkness, when she said, "I'm not a ghost chaser, you know."

That was the first time I'd heard that term. It definitely wasn't the last.

"Ghost chaser?" I said.

"Yeah," she said. "You know."

I waited for a while for her to go on. Instead, she ran her hand up my back and nipped at my ear hard enough to make me wince.

"No," I said. "I do not."

"Oh," she said. "Well, you know there's a bunch of Natalists on this boat, right?"

I scowled. "Yeah, I'm aware. That's one of the reasons I keep to myself so much."

"Well," she said. "Not all of them want you to keep to yourself."

I twisted around until our foreheads were touching. "What?"

She kissed me. "How many women have you been with on this trip?"

"I don't know," I said. "A few?"

She kissed me again. "All of them since the collision, right? All of them since you went through the tank?"

I didn't answer. It was pretty obvious that she knew.

"Ghost chasers," she said. "To a Natalist, you're some serious forbidden fruit. I've heard them talking."

"But that's not you."

"No," she whispered. "That's not me."

IT'S KIND OF tough to date on a colony ship. There just aren't a lot of options, activity-wise. You can eat together, but sucking

food out of a plastic bulb while attached to a tether in the mess
so that you don't float into somebody else who is also sucking
food out of a plastic bulb is even less romantic than it sounds.
You can take walks together, but the only place where walking is
possible is around the carousel, and you spend most of your time
there slightly nauseous while you put more time and attention to
avoiding the squat thrusters than you do to your date. You can
star-watch at the forward viewing ports, but I couldn't do that
without thinking about the stream of high-energy protons flow-
ing past, and what they would do to me—again—if something
happened to one of the field generation units. PTSD-related panic
attacks are also not romantic.

So mostly, we banged.

When we weren't doing that, we spent a lot of time talking.
Nasha had stories. Her parents were immigrants, which, given
the colossal expense and time required to get anywhere in the
Union, is something that almost nobody other than beachhead
colonists can say. They'd come to Midgard thirty years earlier on
the *Lost Hope,* a refugee ship from New Hope, the world that
had been, up until its inhabitants decided to kill one another,
Midgard's nearest neighbor.

You wouldn't think a place like Midgard would be hard on immigrants. It's not like we didn't have the room or resources to take
in a few hundred lost souls. You'd be wrong, though. Humans
are tribal, and the refugees' accents were enough to mark them
as outsiders, even setting aside the fact that the majority of them
had skin a few shades darker than most of Midgard's original
population. They hadn't been on Midgard for a month before
anonymous articles started popping up on the feeds arguing that
they were carriers for whatever lunacy had engulfed New Hope,
and that if they were allowed to insinuate themselves into our social and political life, they'd drag Midgard down that same path.

The government set them up with basic stipends and places to live, but right from the jump it was almost impossible for them to find real jobs. Two years after they landed, a few dozen of them staged a sit-in that turned into a protest that turned into a minor riot. After that, they had a hard time even getting their kids admitted into the general schools.

It was right about then that Nasha was born.

Nasha never told me much about her childhood, but she dropped enough pieces here and there for me to figure out that it was rough. She was pretty up-front about why she learned to fly, though. She'd known since she was a kid that this mission was coming, and she wanted to be on it. She couldn't get into the kind of academic track that would have ended with a doctorate in exobiology, and she didn't have the connections that would have landed her a slot in Security or Command—but she could learn how to pilot a combat skimmer. Killing stuff was the one thing the people from New Hope were good at, right?

"Midgard was never my home," she said to me one night as we curled around one another in her sleeping mesh. "It was never going to be. This place where we're going, though . . ."

"It'll be good," I said. "Warm breezes and white sand beaches, and nothing that wants to eat us."

Famous last words, right?

I WAS WITH Nasha and maybe twenty or thirty other people in the forward common room when we finally shut down the main torch and switched over to ion thrusters for orbital insertion around Niflheim. We hadn't been able to make any kind of observations of our new home yet through the glare of our own exhaust, and everyone was pretty excited to finally see where we were going. A free-fall warning popped up in our oculars, and then thirty seconds later our weight eased away, and we drifted free of the deck.

A minute or so after that, an image of the planet we'd crossed almost eight lights to colonize popped up on the main wallscreen.

Someone up front tried to start a cheer. That died away almost before it began.

I don't know what we were expecting. Green continents and blue oceans? City lights?

What we saw was white. We were still several million klicks out, but from here the planet looked like a pog-ball—smooth, white, and featureless.

"Is that . . ." someone said. "Is that . . . clouds?"

We watched in silence as our maneuvering and the planet's rotation slowly shifted our viewpoint. Nothing changed. After what felt like hours but was probably actually more like ten minutes, Nasha said, "That's not cloud cover. It's ice. This planet's a snowball."

We were holding hands then, mostly just to keep from drifting apart. I squeezed her fingers. She squeezed mine back. I was thinking about all those stories I'd read about colonies that had failed to take root for one reason or another. This didn't look like the sort of place that would welcome us with open arms, but maybe . . .

I pulled her close, and brought my mouth next to her ear.

"This is doable," I said. "Old Earth was like this once, just before life took off. There's plenty of water here, and an oxygen-nitrogen atmosphere. That's all we really need."

She sighed, and turned her head to kiss my cheek.

"I hope so. I'd hate to come all this way just to die."

Those words were still hanging in the air between us when my ocular pinged.

<Command1>:Report to Biology immediately. Come prepared to deploy.

IT'S HARD TO get back to sleep under the best of circumstances after that creepy-ass *out on the hull* dream. With Eight crammed into the bed next to me, wriggling around and mumbling in his sleep, it's impossible. After a half hour or so of trying, I give up and slip out of bed, grab my tablet from my desk, and head down to the caf to do some reading. The corridors are deserted this early except for the occasional Security goon, and I've got the place to myself when I get there. I pick a table in the corner opposite the entrance. On the off chance that someone else wanders in while I'm down here, I'd rather they just left me alone.

My stomach starts rumbling as soon as I sit down. Apparently it knows this is where we go to eat. I'd love to oblige it, but my ration card is zeroed out, and it won't reset until 08:00, which is still a couple of hours away. Downside? I may digest my own liver by then. Upside? I've got plenty of time now to learn a bunch of stuff I don't actually want to know about some colony that crashed and burned in an interesting way somewhere, without being interrupted.

I'm not in the middle of anything right now, so I spend a few minutes browsing through the archives. Nothing's really grabbing me, though, and eventually, out of curiosity, I pull up a file on New Hope. I haven't dug into that particular story since I started my doom-and-gloom tour of the history of the Diaspora—mostly because, like everyone who's lived on Midgard for the past thirty years, I already have a general idea of what happened there.

New Hope failed about twenty-five years after their initial beachhead was established, mostly because of a short, brutal civil war fought between the remaining original colonists and the first wave of the New Hope–born that wrecked most of the infrastructure they still needed in order to survive on a semi-hostile planet. A group of refugees, all from the younger cohort, managed to boost up to the original colony ship that brought them there, which was, like ours here on Niflheim, mostly still in orbit around the planet. They stripped it down to the bare minimum needed to sustain them for a five-year hop—no embryos, no terraforming gear, no Agricultural Section—nothing but life support, a cycler, and a bare minimum of feedstock, basically. They even cut away most of the remaining living space.

When they were done, the ship massed less than ten percent of what the *Drakkar* did when it boosted out. Between the residual fuel that had been left in the ship's tanks, and the antimatter they managed to scavenge from the colony's wrecked power plant, they had just enough juice to limp across the gap to Midgard, where they were welcomed with slightly less than open arms.

As I start reading, it slowly dawns on me that the details the article is filling in give the story a significantly different valance than the one I'd picked up in school. They'd glossed over the reasons for the war, and I'd always assumed it was over the kind of stuff that civil wars are usually over—race, religion, resources, political philosophy, blah blah blah. According to this piece, though, the stated *casus belli* was the question of whether a native corvidlike avian species was sentient, and therefore deserving of protection and respect, or delicious, and therefore deserving of a spicy dry rub and an hour on the grill.

I guess I can see why that wouldn't get a lot of mention. If a colony can go down over something like that, we're all only one step from the corpse hole. I'm not sure what lesson to take from the story, though . . . except maybe that once things start to spiral, it can be really hard to pull them back.

I'm counting down the last ten minutes until I can show the scanner my ocular and draw a mug of cycler paste with equal parts anticipation and disgust when I get a ping from HR. It's my duty cycle for the day. They're seconding me out to Security. I need to be at Lock Two by 08:30, suited up and armed for perimeter patrol.

This sounds like a job for Eight.

I'm just about to tell him this when he pings me instead.

<Mickey8>:Hey Seven. You on your way to the lock?

<Mickey8>:Actually, I kind of thought you might take duty today. You know, considering I almost got eaten while you were napping yesterday.

<Mickey8>:I mean, I would, but . . .

<Mickey8>:Come on, Eight. You owe me.

<Mickey8>:Disagree, friend. If you'll recall, I'm the one who magnanimously did not shove you face-first down the corpse hole after I won our death match of rock-paper-scissors fair and square. Seems to me that you're the one with a debt to repay. Also, I haven't had time to get breakfast yet. You get this one. I'll pick up whatever they assign us to tomorrow.

I'm composing my response, which is definitely going to begin with, *Look, asshole,* when a second window pops open.

<CChen0197>:Hi Mickey. Saw you were on our roster this morning. They've got me on perimeter too. Want to partner? I feel like we made a pretty good team yesterday, right?

I'm trying to decide how to answer that when Eight comes back again.

<Mickey8>:Well, that decides it, huh? I have no idea what shenanigans you and Chen got up to yesterday. Five minutes of talking to me and we'd be outed, right? Right. So, I'm going back to sleep now, okay? Let me know how it goes.

He closes the window. I think about reopening it, and also about storming up there and dragging him out of bed and down to the lock by his ankles, but . . .

But the truth is, he's right.

<CChen0197>:You there?
<Mickey8>:Hi Cat. Yeah, I'm here. Just getting some breakfast before heading over. I'll see you in twenty.

"So," CAT SAYS. "No to the armor, yes to the accelerator, right?"

I look up from strapping on my snowshoes, shake my head, and go back to my laces.

"I'm not telling you what to do, Cat. Dugan was right yesterday. You guys have a different incentive structure than I do."

"Incentive structure?" Cat says. "You mean like the incentive to not get pulled to shreds by those things out there?"

"Yeah," I say. "That one."

I stand, shuffle away from the bench I'd been sitting on, and stomp my feet to make sure the shoes are secure. Cat's geared up the same way I am, with three layers of white camo thermals, snowshoes, and a rebreather pushed up to her forehead. Our weapons are still racked, but she's right about those too. Particularly after yesterday, I'm definitely carrying an accelerator.

"I don't think I buy that," she says. "I saw you yesterday. You didn't want to get pulled down any more than the rest of us did. I know you're supposed to be immortal, but you don't act like you believe it."

I give her a long look, then shrug and shuffle over to the weapons rack. "Have you ever shoved your hand into a shredder?"

She laughs. "What? No."

I pull an accelerator down from the wall, verify that it's powered, and check the load. "Why not? It wouldn't kill you, and the prosthetic they'd give you would be stronger than your real hand. A few hours in Medical and you'd be better than new."

"Oh," she says. "I see where you're going with this."

"You got it," I say. "Even if I don't believe it's permanent, I'm really not interested in dying any more often than I have to. Dying hurts." I shoulder the accelerator and pull on my gloves. "That said, I've got a theory about the creepers. I don't think they're going after us. I think they're after our metal, just like the natives on Roanoke were after their water. If I'm right, wearing combat armor out there is like walking into a wolf's den wrapped in bacon."

"Metal?" Cat says. "They're animals, Mickey. What would they want with metal?"

I shrug. "Who knows? Maybe they're not animals."

Cat pulls down a weapon for herself. "I don't like that. Let's get back to immortality. Do you?"

I look over at her. "Do I what?"

She rolls her eyes. "Believe that you're immortal, Mickey."

I sigh. "Ever heard of the Ship of Theseus?"

She pauses to think. "Maybe? Was that the one that they used to settle Eden?"

"No," I say. "It was not. The Ship of Theseus was a wooden sailing vessel from old Earth days. It got wrecked and had to be rebuilt . . . or else it didn't, I guess, but it still needed to get fixed—"

"Wait," Cat says. "A sailing vessel? Like on the water?"

"Yeah. Theseus sailed around the world in this boat, and it either got wrecked or it didn't, but either way he had to fix it."

"I'm confused. Is this a Schrödinger's cat kind of thing?"

"A what?"

"Schrödinger's cat," she says. "You know, with the box and the poison gas? Quantum superposition and all that?"

"What? No. I told you, it's a boat, not a cat."

"I heard you," she says. "I didn't think your boat was a cat. I'm just saying, it's the same kind of thing, right?"

I have to stop and think about that. For a second it seems like she's actually making sense.

Only for a second, though.

"No," I say. "Not at all. Why would you think that?"

Cat opens her mouth to answer, but before she can, the inner door to the air lock cycles open, and the bored-looking goon sitting beside it waves us over.

"Chen. Barnes. You're up."

"We'll finish this later," Cat says.

We pull down our rebreathers. Cat checks my seals, and I check hers.

"This thing cycles in ten seconds whether you're in it or not," the goon says.

Cat shoulders her weapon, and we go.

"This is bullshit," Cat says.

I look back at her. She's not using the comm, and the combination of the rebreather and Niflheim's atmosphere makes her voice higher than it should be, harsh and tinny. We're walking the perimeter now, shuffling along in our snowshoes, moving from pylon to pylon looking for signs of incursion. There are two other teams out here, spaced equidistant around the kilometer-wide ring that defines the human presence on this planet. We're supposed to keep moving at a steady pace, each team circling the perimeter twice in a six-hour shift. Every time we pass a pylon, it notes our presence and updates our oculars on the positions of the other teams.

"Which part?" I say. "The part where we spend our entire day freezing our asses off walking circles around the dome? Or the part where we maybe get shredded by creepers for no particular good reason?"

"Neither," Cat says. "Walking is good for you, and I guess getting shredded is part of the job when you sign on as Security. What's bullshit is this." She swings her arm in a gesture that takes in everything around us—from the dome, to the snow, to the mountains off in the distance. "This place was supposed to be habitable, remember? Goldilocks zone, oxygen-nitrogen atmosphere, yada yada." She kicks a clump of snow into the air, then watches as it breaks apart into a powdery cloud, glittering in the low yellow sun as it falls back to the ground. "This is not freaking habitable, Mickey. This is, in fact, bullshit."

I open my mouth to start in about the place Asher's World sent her people to. At least this planet didn't kill us dead right away. She turns away and starts walking, though, and I think better of it. I'm not the most sensitive person, but I've been alive long enough to figure out that telling a miserable person about how much worse things could be is usually a bad idea.

The pylons are spaced out at hundred-meter intervals around the perimeter. When we shuffle up to the next one, my ocular pings to let me know that we're moving more quickly than the other two teams, and that we need to slow down by ten percent.

"Ugh," Cat says. "How much slower can we go?"

"They're probably in full armor," I say. "No snowshoes. Remember how much fun that was yesterday?"

"Right. Still, though."

My ocular pings again. Command wants us to wait here for twelve minutes before proceeding. Cat sighs, leans back against the pylon, and sights down along the length of her accelerator, aiming toward a knob of bare rock jutting up out of the snow fifty or so meters away.

"I haven't fired one of these things since basic, back on Midgard," she says. "Hope I still remember how it works."

"Point and click," I say. "The targeting software does most of the work, and the size of the exit wound does the rest."

Her weapon whirs and slams back against her shoulder, and an instant later the top of the rock explodes into a cloud of powdered granite.

"Yeah," she says. "I guess it works."

I'm about to say something about maybe saving her rounds for when we need them when the debris around the rock settles out.

There's a creeper crouched there, head poking up just where Cat's round struck, rear segments trailing back into the snow. Its mandibles are spread wide, and its feeding arms are beckoning.

"Cat?" I say.

"Hush," she says. "I see it."

She aims carefully, and again the accelerator whirs and kicks. The creeper's front segments vanish in a hail of shrapnel, and the body drops back into the snow.

"Yeah," she says. "It definitely works."

The snow around the rock begins to churn.

The disturbance spreads like a wave, snow heaving up and settling back, then heaving again.

It sweeps toward us.

"Mickey?" Cat says.

A creeper breaks through the snow maybe thirty meters off. Cat aims and fires, but it's a panicky shot that raises a gout of steam and snow, but leaves the creeper untouched. The burner on the pylon we're standing under comes to life. Its beam plays across the snow around the rock, and an instant later those from the pylons to our left and right join in. Steam rises in boiling clouds, obscuring my view of the oncoming wave. I've brought my weapon to bear by now, but before I can fire, my field of view splits. My right eye is sighting down the length of my accelerator at where I'm guessing the leading creepers are swarming forward. My left eye, though, is looking back at the dome from a distance. I see the rock Cat destroyed, and the billows of steam where the burners are vaporizing the snow. The images are distorted, colors washed out and features flattened.

Through a break in the steam clouds, I catch a glimpse of two stick-figure humans staring back at me.

I squeeze my eyes shut, but now all I can see is the stylized view coming through my ocular. I must be catching a feed from one of the pylons, maybe? I shake my head and take a half step back. My left snowshoe catches, and I feel myself start to fall. In the view from my ocular, one of the stick figures drops its cartoon rifle and staggers backward as the other turns its balloon head to stare back at me. I'm flailing now and toppling, but my point of view doesn't shift as the disarmed stick figure disappears into the pixelated snow. The other raises its weapon and fires again and again, each shot producing an explosion in the mid-distance between it and me.

I can hear voices, but I can't separate the shouting over the comm from Cat's bellowing rage from something else, something calmer and quieter but not quite understandable. The remaining stick figure raises its aim point, and its line-drawing rifle shrinks down to a dot . . .

"HE'S COMING AROUND."

The voice is unfamiliar. It takes me a long moment to realize that it's referring to me.

"Can he hear us?"

That's Cat. I open my eyes to find myself flat on my back in an exam cube somewhere in Medical. Cat is leaning over me. She looks worried.

"Hey," she says. "You in there?"

It takes me a few seconds to scare up enough saliva to speak.

"Yeah," I say finally. "I'm in here. What happened?"

Cat straightens, and I try to sit up. Hands grasp my shoulders from behind, though, and gently press me back down.

"Easy, Barnes. Let's make sure you're functioning before we try moving too much."

I look back, and find myself gazing up into the white-haired nostrils of a middle-aged, balding medico named Burke.

I don't find his presence all that reassuring. He's killed me several times.

"Sorry," I say. "Is there something wrong with me?"

"Don't know," Burke says. "I can't find any sign of physical trauma, and your EEG looks normal at the moment. From what Chen tells me, though, you dropped like a sack of flour for no obvious reason out there. That's generally not a great sign from a medical standpoint."

"Why aren't we dead? The creepers were coming for us, weren't they?"

"They were," Cat says. "I don't know why they stopped."

"The pylons," I say. "They were firing, right?"

"Yeah," Cat says. "The burners on the pylons are a lot more powerful than the man-portable ones. There weren't any dead creepers lying around when the steam cleared, but maybe they forced them to ground?"

"Maybe," I say. For some reason, though, I don't think so.

"Or," Cat says, "maybe I got the boss creeper."

I shrug out from under Burke's hands and sit up. "What?"

"After the pylons kicked in, I couldn't see what was happening in front of us. Too much steam, you know? So I looked up, and a bit up the hillside there was this gigantic creeper reared up out of the snow."

That gets my attention. "How gigantic?"

She shrugs. "Hard to say. It was at least a hundred meters off. Maybe twice the size of the other ones? Maybe more? Anyway, it was the only target I could actually get a bead on, so I popped it. A few seconds later, the pylons shut down, and the creepers were gone."

I swing my legs over the side of the table. "How many mandibles did it have?"

Cat's eyebrows come together at the bridge of her nose. "None, after I popped it. Before that? I didn't stop to count."

I get to my feet. The world swims briefly, then comes back into focus.

"You should stick around for a while," Burke says. "Neurological events like this are no joke, Barnes. I'd like to get some imaging done. You might have a tumor."

I shoot him a look, then shake my head and pick up my shirt from the swivel chair where someone apparently tossed it when they brought me in.

"I don't have a tumor," I mutter.

"You don't know that," Burke says.

"We've had this conversation before," I say. "Don't you remember? Tumors take a long time to grow, and I've only been alive for a day and a half."

He winces. I guess he does remember.

"Fine," he says. "It's not a tumor. Let me check one more thing, though."

He turns to rummage in a drawer, and pulls out a slim wand with what looks like a suction cup on one end and a readout on the other. He comes over to me as I'm pulling my shirt on over my head and puts one hand on my shoulder.

"Hold still," he says, "and look up at the ceiling."

I let my breath out in a put-upon sigh and roll my eyes up as far as they'll go. Burke cups the back of my head with one hand, and presses the tip of the wand against my left eye.

"Ouch."

"Oh, don't be a baby. This will only take a second."

The wand beeps, and he pulls it away. "Huh," he says.

Cat steps forward and peers over his shoulder at the readout. "What does that mean?"

He turns to look at her. "Looks like there's been a power surge in his ocular sometime in the past hour. You should get that checked, Barnes. Those things have a direct connection to your brain, you know. A fritzing ocular is dangerous."

"Okay," I say. "Can you check it?"

He shakes his head. "I only handle wetware. You need someone from Bioelectronics."

Of course.

"Thanks," I say. "I'll be sure to get right on that."

"So," CAT SAYS. "What actually happened to you out there, Mickey?"

We're in the first-level main corridor now, near the cycler. I understand why that and Medical are co-located, but it still gives me the creeps as we walk past the entrance.

"No idea," I say. "I just blacked out."

Did I, though? The memory of seeing cartoon-me and cartoon-Cat is starting to feel more and more like the sort of thing an electroshocked brain would come up with just before shutting down, but . . .

"I would say you should see a doctor," Cat says, "but I guess you just did, huh? Are you going to try to get in to see somebody about your ocular, like Burke said?"

"Maybe," I say. "I've got some stuff I need to take care of this afternoon, but I'll see if I can get an appointment with somebody tomorrow if I have a chance."

"Sounds like something you might want to get looked at sooner than later, but I guess it's your call."

"Thanks," I say. "I'll give it some thought."

This is a lie. I've already done all the thinking I need to do on this topic. Like Burke said, ocular implants are interwoven with our optic nerves, and they interface with our brains in a half dozen other places. You can't just snap one out and snap another one in. Anybody else with a glitching ocular would be in for a long, tricky microsurgery to install a replacement unit.

Somehow, I don't think they'd spare that kind of effort for me. Easier to just give me a trip to the tank.

We've reached the central stairs. I take one step up, then turn to look back. Cat isn't following.

"I've still got three hours on shift," she says. "Amundsen said I could make sure you were okay, but I've got to get back now."

"Oh," I say. "Do they need me?"

Cat gives me a half smile. "After what just happened? No. Not now, and probably not anytime soon. Security isn't too keen on people who faint under fire."

Ouch.

"I didn't faint," I say. "I glitched. I was picking something up . . ."

She raises one eyebrow. "Picking something up?"

"Yeah," I say. "I was . . ."

It suddenly occurs to me that I might not want to tell Cat what I was seeing when I went down out there. I don't want her to think I'm breaking down.

I don't want to think about what it means if I'm *not* breaking down.

"I don't know," I say. "Something weird happened, for sure, but I definitely didn't just faint."

Cat looks uncomfortable now. "It's okay, Mickey. You wouldn't be the first person to panic under fire."

"Is that what you think happened?"

She looks away. "Doesn't matter what I think, does it? I'll see you later, Mickey."

AFTER I LEAVE Cat, I stop by the caf for another shot of cycler paste, then head back up to my rack. What else can I do? When I get there, I find Eight sitting up in bed, our tablet propped on his knees.

"Hey," he says. "You're back early."

I drop into our chair and start unlacing my boots. "Got attacked again. Almost died again. Wound up in Medical this time. They said I should go home and tell you to start doing your share of this bullshit from now on."

Eight sets the tablet aside, stretches, and gets to his feet. "Uh-huh. Well, since you're back, I'm gonna go get myself something to eat. How much of our ration did you leave me?"

"Not sure," I say. "Maybe nine hundred kcal?"

"Great," he says. "I'm taking it all."

I start to protest, but he's already on his way out the door.

"Don't even," he says without looking back. "I just came out of the tank."

"Hey," I say to his retreating back. "Put the wrap back on your wrist, huh?"

He pulls up his sleeve to show me. It's there, but it's not even on straight. I open my mouth to say something, but he cuts me off with an eye roll.

"Don't worry," he says. "If anyone asks, I'll tell them I'm a quick healer."

When he's gone, I crawl into bed and pick up the tablet. He'd been reading about Asher's World. I spend five seconds wondering at the fact that he's perseverating over the exact same stuff that I am before I remember that the surprising thing would be if he weren't, considering that he's basically me, to within a rounding error.

Well, me minus the past six weeks or so, anyway. For some reason, that seems to have made an increasingly big difference.

I've been giving this some thought, and here's the thing about the Asher's World expedition: Their situation wasn't actually all that different from ours. Their target planet was too hot to support life. This one isn't quite too cold, but it's close. A better reading on the O_2 levels in the atmosphere might have clued the mission planners back on Midgard in to the fact that the biosphere on Niflheim is barely hanging on, but I guess at seven-plus lights distance you get what you get.

I can't help wondering what we'd have done if this place had been just a little bit worse—a few degrees colder, a bit less oxygen, something really toxic in the atmosphere, maybe? We brought terraforming gear, but that's an insanely slow process. I've read about dozens of colonies that faced similar predicaments. Some tried to regroup, refuel, and reach for another target. Some tried to hunker down in orbit, drop their terraformers, and make it work.

Some, like the folks from Asher's World, just gave up and called it a day.

Of the ones that kept trying, I could count on one hand the number that actually succeeded. Seeding a colony is hard on a hospitable planet. On an inhospitable one, it's damn near impossible.

And what about one like Niflheim? Time will tell, I guess.

I'm pondering that question, and thinking about what it'll mean for me if things go south here, when my ocular pings.

<RedHawk>:Hey Mick. I heard you had a rough day today. I'm off shift at 16:00. Want to meet for dinner? My treat.

The answer is, *Hell, yes,* but that's competing in my head with, *How the shit can you afford to spring for dinner?* and before I can sort that out and formulate an answer, another message pops up.

<Mickey8>:Absolutely. See you then, pal.

Oh *hell* no. I open up a private window.

<Mickey8>:No you don't, Eight. This one's mine.
<Mickey8>:Tank funk, Seven. I need real food. There's still three hundred kcal on our card for the day. You can have it back.
<Mickey8>:Look, friend. I've almost died twice in the past twenty-four hours, and you were napping both times. If you want to push this, we can meet back at the cycler in twenty and go for real this time.
<Mickey8>:Wow. That escalated quickly.
<Mickey8>:No joke, Eight. If you're not back here by 15:45, it's go time.
<Mickey8>:...
<Mickey8>:So?
<Mickey8>:Fine. Fine. Have your fancy dinner, you big baby. Man, I cannot wait until you get eaten.

"Go nuts," Berto says. "Anything you want, buddy."

My eyes drift to the rabbit.

"Within reason," he adds. "I'm not made of kcal, you know."

I glance around the caf. We're on the early side for dinner, so it's not too crowded yet. There's a bunch of Security types at one table near the door, though. One of them meets my eyes. He says something to his friends, and the table bursts out laughing.

Great. Now I'm the Expendable who's afraid to die. I'm pretty sure that's as low as you can sink in terms of social standing around here.

"Hey," Berto says. "You still with me?"

I turn back to the service counter. "Give me a limit," I say. "I could literally eat everything they have back there."

Berto looks down at the counter and scratches the back of his head. "Tell you what. Keep it under a thousand kcal, okay?"

I stare up at him. "A thousand? Seriously?"

"Yeah," he says. "I meant what I said before, buddy. You're my best friend. I shouldn't have lied to you. I guess this is my way of apologizing."

He's still lying to me, but at this moment I don't remotely care. I order potatoes, fried crickets, and a tiny bowl of chopped lettuce and tomatoes. That only comes to seven hundred kcal, so I top it off with a mug of paste. Waste not, want not, right? As my tray slides out of the dispenser, I see that Berto's ordering as well.

He gets the rabbit.

"Berto?" I say. "What the hell, friend?"

He grins. "You didn't think I was starving myself for you, did you? Come on, Mickey. I feel bad, but not that bad. This isn't me flagellating myself. It's more of a share-the-wealth kind of thing."

Our total is twenty-four hundred kcal. Berto shows his ocular to the scanner. It flashes green.

"Seriously," I say. "What. The. Hell."

Berto's grin widens. "You remember when I took you out in the flitter?"

Oh God, do I remember.

"Yeah," I say. "I think so."

His tray pops out. We gather our food and head toward a table in the back. I can feel the Security guys' eyes on the back of my neck as we go.

"Remember when we swung out over that ridge line, about twenty klicks south of the dome?"

That whole trip is actually a blur, and I have no idea what he's talking about, but in the interest of moving the story along, I nod. We sit, and he immediately tears into his rabbit haunch.

"There was a rock formation at the top of the ridge," he says around a mouthful of meat. "We flew right over it. Do you remember?"

At this point, I think we've reached the limits of bullshit. "No," I say. "I honestly don't."

He shrugs. "Doesn't matter. Picture a spike of granite, maybe thirty meters tall, with another slab just a little shorter leaning against it. The space between is maybe ten meters at the base, tapering down to nothing at the top."

"Okay," I say. "I guess I can picture that." Actually, now that he's described it, I think I do remember seeing the place he's talking about. I thought at the time that it might be a good spot for bouldering.

That was before the creepers, obviously.

"Right," Berto says. "So for the last few weeks I've been telling anybody who would listen that I thought I could get the flitter through the gap. Crazy, right? I mean, even rolled ninety degrees, the clearance on either side would be like half a meter at the top end, and you'd have to initiate the roll with a margin of maybe a tenth of a second."

"Yeah," I say. "That does sound crazy. So?"

"So," Berto says, "everybody else thought it was crazy too. I've been collecting bets."

He stops there to take a bite, but I don't need him to finish that thought.

"You did it?"

"Yeah," he says, with a grin that I don't think I've seen since he won that goddamned pog-ball tournament. "I did. I collected three thousand kcal, all told. Sweet, right?"

"You . . ." I begin, then have to stop to collect myself. "You could have died, Berto."

"Could have," he says. "Didn't."

I set my fork down beside my tray, and my hands clench into fists. "You risked your life. You risked your fucking life for two days' rations."

His smug grin fades. "Hey," he says. "Easy, there, buddy. It wasn't that big a deal."

"Not a big deal? You risked your life for goddamned *kcal*, Berto. You wouldn't risk jack fucking shit for me."

Berto's face goes slack. He stares at me. I stare back.

This is the point where I realize that I've just told him something that I'm not supposed to know . . . or, wait, did I? Good lord, I can't keep track of my own lies at this point, let alone Berto's.

"Mickey?" Berto says. "What do you mean by that, exactly?"

I open my mouth to reply, then let it fall closed again.

"You just came out of the tank," he says. "Isn't that right, Mickey?"

I look away. One of the Security guys is staring at us.

"Yeah, Berto. You know I did."

"I thought I did," Berto says. "Gotta admit, though. You're making me wonder."

I stab a potato, bring it to my mouth, and chew. This meal is the first solid food I've eaten in over two days. It's a sin that I'm not enjoying this as much as I should be. Over the course of five seconds I decide to come clean with him and then change my mind again a half dozen times. When I look back at Berto, he's chewing slowly and watching me through narrowed eyes. *I didn't die,* I picture myself saying. *You left me in that fucking crevasse, but I didn't die.* As he takes another bite of rabbit, I imagine adding, *Maybe I should have offered you a couple days' rations to come back for me, huh?* I'm working my way up to actually opening my mouth and saying it when the goon who's been watching us gets up from his table and starts over toward ours.

I know this guy, vaguely at least. His name is Darren. He's big for a colonist, almost as tall as Berto and probably ten kilos heavier, with close-cut dark hair and a weird curly tuft of beard growing from the bottom of his chin. He's not stupid—nobody who was selected for this expedition is stupid—but he's always struck me as having the kind of attitude that dumb guys get when you give them just a little bit of power. He stops a pace or two behind Berto, folds his arms across his chest, and tilts his head to one side.

"Hey," he says. "You gentlemen enjoying our rations tonight?"

Berto turns to look, then brings the rabbit haunch to his mouth and takes a slow, deliberate bite.

"Yeah," he says with his mouth still full. "Very much, actually."

Darren's face twists into a scowl. "You're an ass, Gomez. You could have wasted yourself and our only functional flitter out there this morning."

Berto shrugs, turns back to me, and takes another bite.

"Flitter's no use without me anyway. Nasha won't fly anything without a gravitic grid." He chews, swallows, and wipes his mouth with his sleeve. "Anyway, if you felt so strongly about protecting colony assets, why'd you put kcal into the pool? I wouldn't have done it if there weren't any stakes." The grin comes back now, and he looks up at me and winks. "Oh, who am I kidding? Sure I would have. This place is boring, and that was a hell of a ride."

A hell of a ride. I just fucking bet it was. My jaw is knotted so tight that it feels like my teeth might crack. Darren's eyes shift to me.

"What's your problem, Barnes?"

I don't trust my voice to answer. Darren's eyebrows come together at the bridge of his nose, and he takes a half step forward.

"Seriously," he says. "If you've got something to say, say it. If you don't, wipe that look off your face."

"Back off," Berto says. "Mickey's had a rough couple of days."

"Yeah," Darren says. "I heard. He got two of our guys killed yesterday, and then today he dipped out of a fight and left Chen to rescue his ass for the second time in twenty-four hours. I feel for you, man."

Berto sets the rabbit bone he'd been gnawing carefully onto

his tray, then puts both hands flat on the table. He's not smirking anymore.

"Step away, Darren."

"Suck it, Gomez. I just ate goddamned cycler paste for dinner, and I'm not in the mood for—"

He stops there, because he's made the extremely poor choice to shove the back of Berto's head. As I said, Darren's a big guy, and he's Security. He's probably used to people letting him get away with that kind of stuff.

Berto, to my knowledge, has never let anyone get away with that kind of stuff.

Berto pushes up from the table and pivots on his back leg, already swinging as the bench he'd been sitting on slams into Darren's shins.

There's a reason Berto is hell at pog-ball. For someone as tall and lanky as he is, he's inhumanly fast. Darren hasn't even managed to get his hands up when Berto's fist smacks into the left side of his face and drops him.

At this point, what had been standard middle-school bullshit turns into a riot.

I'm up and coming around the table as Darren tries to get back to his feet. He makes it as far as one knee before Berto puts a foot to his shoulder and shoves him back down. Berto still has one foot in the air when the first of the goons from Darren's table slams into him and drives him facedown onto our table hard enough that I have to jump back to keep from being knocked down as it slides a half meter across the floor under the impact. Berto tries to wriggle free, but two more are on him now, kicking his legs out from under him and pinning his arms behind his back. I manage to get my good hand on one of their shoulders before someone grabs me by the collar, yanks me off my feet, slams me facedown onto the floor, and plants a knee in the middle of my back. The last thing I feel is the tines of a Taser pressed against the back of my neck.

"EXPLAIN YOURSELVES."

I glance over at Berto. He's staring at a spot on the wall behind Marshall's head. After an awkward five seconds of silence, I say, "This was a bit of a misunderstanding, sir."

Marshall closes his eyes and visibly unclenches his jaw. When he opens them again, they're narrowed to slits.

"A misunderstanding," he says. "Is that how you would characterize the events of this afternoon, Mr. Gomez?"

"No, sir," Berto says. "I believe everyone involved understood what was happening quite clearly."

"I see," Marshall says. "And what, exactly, was this thing that everyone so clearly understood?"

Berto can't keep a hint of a smile from creeping onto his face.

"Primarily that the Security officers involved were upset about the consequences of their own poor judgment, and one of them decided to work out his frustrations by assaulting an innocent bystander."

"Huh," Marshall says. "Mr. Drake assaulted you? How is it, then, that he's in Medical with a cracked zygomatic arch, while you appear to be completely uninjured?"

Berto shrugs. "I said he assaulted me. I didn't say he did a good job of it."

Marshall's scowl deepens, and he turns to me. "Do you agree with the way Gomez is characterizing this incident, Mr. Barnes?"

"Basically, yes," I say. "Darren came over to talk to us on his own. We weren't even looking at him. He was clearly pretty upset about having to eat cycler paste for dinner, and it seemed like he was hoping to start something with me over it. Once things got going he did seem to be a bit surprised, but I'm not sure why he should have been. I mean, he did lay hands on Berto first."

Marshall's face twists into a *just ate dog shit* grimace.

"Yes, well. I'd like to come down on you over this, especially since this is the second time I've had the two of you in my office in the past twenty-four hours. Unfortunately, however, surveillance video appears to back up your claim for the most part. Drake clearly approached you unsolicited, and he does appear to have at least touched Gomez prior to being coldcocked. Honestly, I expect better from our Security team." He doesn't clarify whether he means better judgment, or better skills at fistfighting. Instead, he leans back in his chair and folds his arms across his chest. "I am curious, though. Why was Drake eating cycler paste while the two of you were enjoying a comparative feast? If I recall correctly, I docked both of your rations yesterday, while he's currently allocated two thousand kcal per day." He strokes his chin thoughtfully. "And regardless of his reasons, why in the world would he have held you responsible?"

Berto shoots me a quick look, but I've got nothing.

"It's hard to say, sir," he says. "Maybe he had a big breakfast?"

"I see," Marshall says. "So it wouldn't have had anything to do with this?"

He taps a tablet lying on his desk, and a video clip pops up in my ocular. I blink to stream. It's a grainy, long-distance view of Berto's flitter diving toward a jumble of rocks piled at the crest of a snowy ridgeline. The formation looks pretty much the way I remember it, with two slabs rising up from a boulder field to form a narrow triangle. From this angle, there doesn't appear to be any possible way that the flitter can fit through the gap, and even though I know what happens, I can feel my stomach clenching. Berto pulls up level about a hundred meters out, adjusts his altitude slightly, and then rolls the plane at the last instant so that it passes through the rocks without so much as scratching the paint.

"Oh," Berto says. "You caught that, huh?"

"Yes," Marshall says. "We caught that. We are in a state of heightened alert at the moment, Gomez. We have been losing people, and we have precious few to spare. As a result, we are keeping an eye on things. There is very little you can do that we won't catch. Now, given that you are aware of our precarious position in terms of both personnel and material resources, would you care to explain why you found it necessary to risk both your own life and, more importantly, two thousand kilos of irreplaceable metal and electronics for what appears to be a juvenile stunt?"

Berto sits silent, eyes fixed on the wall. Marshall stares him down for what feels like a very long time.

"Fine," Marshall says finally. "I'm aware of your wager, obviously. I don't suppose there's any point in explaining to you all the regulations you've violated in the past two days, because you clearly don't care." He leans forward, plants his elbows on his desk, and sighs. "At this point, I'm not sure what to do with you, Gomez. I can't afford to ground you, which honestly is the very least that you deserve, and sadly flogging is not an approved disciplinary technique under standard Union guidelines." He pauses then, and turns to me. "Barnes—do you have any suggestions?"

I glance quickly at Berto, then back to Marshall. "Me, sir? No, sir."

Marshall sighs again, and leans back in his chair. "Given my limited options, I suppose the best I can do is increase your workload and cut your rations. You'll cover Adjaya's shifts aloft as well as your own for the next five days, Gomez. That should keep you out of trouble, at the least. In addition, I'm reducing your rations a further ten percent. That shouldn't bother you, as you won't have time to eat in any case. I'm also blocking your ability to accept transfers from any other personnel, just in case you have any more ideas for scamming your fellow colonists."

"Sir—" Berto begins, but Marshall cuts him off before he can even finish that first syllable.

"Don't waste your breath, Gomez. As I said, this is the absolute *least* that you deserve. If you press me on this, you may force me to examine more radical solutions to the problem you present."

Berto looks like he has more to say, but with a visible struggle he swallows, fixes his eyes back on that spot behind Marshall's head, and says, "Yes, sir. Thank you, sir."

"Excellent," Marshall says. "Go." As we rise and turn to leave, he says, "Oh, Barnes? I don't know what your involvement in this incident was, but on the presumption that you probably had something to do with it, I'll be reducing your rations by five percent as well."

I turn back to him. "What? No!"

"Ten percent," Marshall says. When I open my mouth again, he says, "Care to make it fifteen?"

My jaw snaps shut with an audible click.

"No, sir," I say. "Thank you, sir."

"ANOTHER TEN PERCENT? Come on, Seven! You can't do that to me!"

"First," I say, "I'm not doing it to *you*. I'm doing it to *us*. And second, *I'm* not doing it. If you want to bitch at somebody, bitch at Berto. He's the one who decided to screw half the Security Section out of their rations and then clock one of them in the caf."

Eight slumps down onto the bed and drops his face into his hands. "I can't do this, Seven. I never got a chance to recover from the tank. You know this body still hasn't eaten a single damned bite of solid food, right? Eating is all I think about from the time I wake up until the time I go to sleep. Now we're down to, what, seven-twenty each? I can't do it. I cannot fucking do it."

"I'm sorry," I say. "Seriously, I know you must be going through hell right now, but look—there's nothing to be done. Unless we want to go back to the corpse hole, we're just going to have to deal with this."

He looks up. "I'm not gonna lie, Seven. The corpse hole is sounding better and better right now."

I drop into the desk chair, pull my boots off, and prop my feet up on the bed beside him. "It might come to that, friend-o, but we're not there yet. Tell you what—you can have whatever's left on our account for today, and I guess . . . nine hundred tomorrow? Does that help?"

He groans.

"Look," I say, "that's only leaving me five-forty for the next thirty-six hours, and I didn't even get to finish my dinner before Berto started his little riot. I know you're dying right now, but this isn't exactly a picnic for me either."

He sighs, and flops over onto his back.

"I know," he says to the ceiling, "I know you're hurting too, and I do appreciate the offer. You're a good guy, Seven. I'm gonna feel terrible when I finally wind up strangling you in your sleep and eating your corpse."

I don't have time to come up with a response to that before my ocular pings.

<Black Hornet>: Hey there. You off-shift?

I start to compose an answer, but Eight beats me to the punch.

<Mickey8>: Yeah. Thought you were flying tonight?

<Black Hornet>:I was, but now I'm not. Looks like they swapped Berto into my slots for the next few days for some reason, so I'm free until further notice. Want to hang?

<Mickey8>: Hells yes!

<Black Hornet>: Sweet. See you in ten.

"Sorry," Eight says. "You gotta go."

"Hey," I begin, but he cuts me off.

"No, Seven. Don't even. I need this. I *need* this. I was mostly joking about strangling you in your sleep, but if you try to fight me on this, I swear that I will end you."

The rage that boils up in me now is completely out of proportion to anything that he said. I recognize that.

I recognize it, but I don't care.

"Look," I say. "I get that you're having a rough go, you big fucking baby, but you're really starting to push it, you know that? I've taken two days of hazard duty while you've been napping up here, and I just offered to give you three-quarters of our rations for the next two days out of the goodness of my dumbass heart. You just came out of the tank, fine, you're hungry—but I'm hungry too, and I almost got killed today, and anyway there's nothing I remember about tank funk that makes us extra-horny. So if you want to keep walking this road, we can head down to Marshall's office together right now and settle this for good."

He stares at me for a long five seconds, his jaw hanging slightly open.

"Wait," he says finally. "What? You think this is a sex thing?"

That sets me back. "Uh . . . yes?"

He groans, sits up, and rubs his face with both hands. "Good God, Seven. Did I not just tell you that I'm starving to death? You think I've got the energy for sex right now? When Nasha gets here, I'm not gonna try to get her out of her jumpsuit, you idiot. I'm gonna try to talk her into feeding me. You got yours from Berto, even if you didn't get all of it down your neck, for some reason. You've got to give me this."

And just like that, the anger drains away.

"Oh," I say. "Right."

"Right. So?"

I stare at him. He stares back. After a few seconds of this, he rolls his eyes and points to the door.

"Right," I say again.

I pull on my boots, and I go.

SO HERE'S A fun story about starvation. Everybody knows Eden was the first colony, right? The first place old Earth successfully infected with her children. Not everybody knows, though, that the mission that dropped the beachhead on Eden was actually our second attempt.

The first, on a ship called the *Ching Shih,* went off almost forty years prior, twenty years or so after the end of the Bubble War. That mission was our species' first desperate attempt at flinging ourselves past our own heliopause—and like most of our first attempts at most things, it didn't go particularly well. The ship didn't have a cycler, and their engines weren't anywhere near as efficient as ours, and Earth to Eden is a long jump even by modern standards. They were expecting to be twenty-one years in transit, and they were expecting to sustain themselves for that entire time with shipboard agriculture.

Given what they were up against, and the primitive state of their technology base, and their woeful ignorance about what the interstellar environment can do to you at relativistic speeds, it's actually pretty impressive that they got as far as they did. They were almost twelve years out when their crops began failing. As far as anyone could tell from their transmissions, they never did fully understand what was happening. The best guess in the account I read was that the plants were suffering from cumulative radiation damage, compounded over multiple generations until there were just too many mutations for the organisms to be viable anymore. The *Ching Shih's* field generators weren't as efficient as ours, and their Agriculture Section was located in the front third of the ship, apparently on the theory that the humans were the ones who really needed the shielding, so those poor plants were taking a serious beating.

The thing about disasters in interstellar space is that some of them are fast, and some of them are slow—but either kind can leave you really, really dead. The *Ching Shih* died slowly. To their credit, they documented the entire process, even when it was clear that their situation was completely hopeless, in the interest of making sure the next mission wouldn't make the same mistakes. They got through most of a year by progressively cutting rations. When it was obvious that wasn't going to be enough, the mission commander put out a standing request for volunteers to be converted from calorie sinks to calorie sources.

Starvation hurts. She got a surprising number of takers.

It took another three years before she finally faced up to the fact that even if she cut the crew down to the minimum needed to keep the ship running, and maybe still be able to unpack their stored embryos at the journey's end, they weren't going to make it. Their Agriculture Section was producing next to nothing by then, and the mission plan had relied on the crops to do a fair bit of their carbon cycling as well as providing food for the crew, so things were falling apart on multiple levels. They were still four years out from Eden when the last twelve crew members powered the ship down, stripped to their underwear, and stepped out of the main air lock.

The *Ching Shih* is still out there somewhere, humming through the void at point-six *c* or so—and so, I suppose, are the bodies of those last twelve would-be colonists. I find myself wondering sometimes if someone somewhere might see them zip by someday and wonder where they're going in such a hurry . . . and why the hell they're not wearing suits.

THE PROBLEM WITH getting kicked out of your room when you live in a rat-warren dome on a planet with a poisonous atmosphere and hostile natives is that there aren't a lot of places to go. We don't have theaters. We don't have coffee shops. We don't have parks, or plazas, or hangouts. What we have, mostly, is workspaces, the majority of which range from unpleasant (sewage reclamation) to hostile (Security's ready room). The Agriculture Section is actually not a bad place to be, if you can avoid getting depressed about the feeble state of most of the growing things, but I'm not welcome there except on days when I've been seconded out to them, so that's a no-go.

For lack of better options, I head down to the caf.

It's on the late side for dinner now, so I don't anticipate finding a big crowd there, but when I walk through the door, it's even more sparse than I expected. There's a group of four at a table near the back, picking over two trays of potatoes between them, and a guy I know vaguely from the Biology Section sitting alone in the opposite corner, nursing what looks like a paste smoothie and staring down at his tablet. His name is Highsmith. He's a history buff of sorts. I once had a fun conversation with him about the parallels between the Diaspora and the original spread of the human species out of Africa on old Earth. Most of his opinions were wrong, but I had a good time telling him exactly why that was so.

I briefly—very briefly—consider asking if he wants company, before realizing first that my ration is zeroed out for the day, and then how weird it would be for me to sit down across from him in the cafeteria with no food of my own and then try to strike up a conversation. Instead, I take a bench at a table near the door, as far from both him and the others as I can get, pull out my own tablet, and start browsing for a distraction.

After ten minutes or so without inspiration, I finally decide to go old school, with an article about the failure of the old Earth Vikings' Greenland colony. Their situation, as it turns out, wasn't all that different from ours in a lot of ways. They tried to build a sustainable society in a cold, inhospitable place where their traditional food crops wouldn't grow. They got into fights with hostile locals. I assume their leader was kind of a jerk.

Eventually, they starved to death.

That last bit takes me back to Eight, lying on our bed moaning about how he's digesting his own liver, and to Nasha, going up there probably expecting a fun time and instead getting him-as-me begging her to buy him something to eat.

Something to eat.

Where would they go to get something to eat?

I'm already on my feet before that thought has a chance to finish forming. Highsmith looks up from his tablet as my bench flips over behind me and I scoot over to the door. How long has it been? And how long would it take Eight to talk Nasha into coming down here? And how long would it take them to make the trip? I don't know the answer to any of those questions exactly, but I can't help but think that they're probably converging rapidly. I ping Eight.

<Mickey8>:Where are you?
<Mickey8>:On our way to the caf. Why?
<Mickey8>:Where, specifically?
<Mickey8>:Bottom of the central stairs. What the hell, Seven?

They'll be coming around the corner in ten seconds.

Maybe less than ten seconds.

It's okay. I've got time. I don't even need to run, really, just fast-walk down the corridor to the next intersection and take a turn. That done, I lean back against the wall, breathe in deep, and let it back out slowly. What if my brain hadn't kicked in when it did? What would have happened if Nasha and Eight had walked into the caf to find me sitting there staring at my tablet?

Come to that, what's Highsmith going to think when he sees

me walking back through the door, twenty seconds after I left in such a hurry, with Nasha beside me?

Ugh. With Nasha, and wearing a different shirt. Hopefully he's not too observant.

Best not to think about that. More importantly, where do I go now?

Can't go back to my room. I think it's probably safe to assume that they'll be headed there as soon as Eight has something in his belly.

I give some brief thought to heading up to Nasha's rack. She shares with a woman from Agriculture named Trudy. Trudy's nice enough. She'd probably let me hang around if I told her I was waiting for Nasha—who would eventually actually show up, and probably wonder how I got from my rack to hers quicker than she did, and what the hell I was doing there anyway.

Yeah, that won't work.

There's really only one other public space in the dome. Fortunately, this one is pretty much guaranteed to be empty more or less all the time.

I sigh, and straighten, and head for the gym.

A WORKOUT CENTER is not standard equipment on a beachhead colony. That we have one is a testament to Hieronymus Marshall's enduring belief in the importance of physical fitness as a component of moral and ethical fitness.

The fact that it is the only space in the dome guaranteed to be empty at any time of day or night is testament to the fact that, despite what Hieronymus Marshall might feel on the topic, exercise is the absolute last thing anyone wants to do during a famine.

The truth is, I don't even know exactly where the gym is. I have to pull up a map of the dome on my ocular to figure it out. Turns out it's right down the corridor from the cycler, which strikes me as oddly appropriate in the moment.

I take the long route around, following one of the spoke corridors to the outer ring and then taking that halfway around the dome before cutting back in, with the idea that I'd be less likely to run into anyone on their way to the caf or to start the new shift in Agriculture. I still pass a half dozen people, though, and I feel like they're all looking at me strangely. Paranoia? Maybe—or maybe they all just saw Eight and Nasha passing by, they've figured out exactly what's going on, and they're pinging Security as soon as I'm out of sight.

We've only been at this for two days now, and I'm already losing it.

When I finally reach the gym, I crack open the door and duck inside like I'm being pursued. I slam the door behind me, close my eyes, and lean my forehead against the cool plastic surface.

"Is there a problem?"

My head snaps around and my heart lurches so hard that for an instant I'm afraid I might be dying. This isn't much of a gym—just a row of treadmills, a rack for pull-ups, and a half dozen dumbbells in a space maybe two or three times the size of my room.

It's not empty.

In fact, there's a woman on one of the treadmills. She's turned around now, feet on the side rails, mat running away beneath her.

It takes me a long second of heart-thudding panic to realize that it's Cat.

We stare each other down. She stops the treadmill, steps down onto the floor, and folds her arms across her chest.

"What are you doing here?" I manage.

She rolls her eyes. "You sure you're the one who should be asking that question?"

I close my eyes and breathe until my pulse settles down to something close to normal. When I open them again, Cat's expression is shading from confusion to concern.

"Sorry," I say. I cross the room in three steps, turn, and lower myself down to sit on the last treadmill in the row. "I'm having a weird day."

"Yeah," she says. "I know. Do you need to go back to Medical? You look a little crazed right now."

"No," I say, maybe a little too quickly. "No. I'm fine. I just wanted a little space to myself, I guess, and you kind of startled me. It never occurred to me that someone might actually be down here working out."

She smiles, drops her arms to her sides, and comes over to sit beside me. "That's fair."

I turn to look at her. Her hair is pulled back into a high ponytail, and she's dressed in the tight gray under-suit from her combat armor. Somehow, she manages to wear it well. She isn't really sweating, so I'm guessing she hasn't been here for long.

"Seriously," I say. "What are you up to down here? You know we're in the middle of a famine, right?"

"Yeah," she says. "I'm aware."

"So?"

She sighs. "Gillian Branch was my bunkmate."

"Oh," I say. "Who's that?"

She shoots me a sharp, angry look. "We're all just anonymous goons to you, huh?"

I lean back, both hands raised in surrender.

"No! No, it's definitely not a you thing. It's a me thing. I don't socialize much with anybody, Cat. A lot of people around here think I'm some kind of abomination, you know? And a lot of the ones who want to talk to me are just looking to play out some weird fetish fantasy. It's just easier most of the time if I keep to myself."

"Oh," she says. "Ghost chasers, huh?"

"Yeah," I say. "You're not . . ."

Her eyes narrow. "Excuse me?"

"Sorry," I say. "It's just . . ."

"I already told you I'm not a Natalist, if that's what you're asking."

"Right," I say. "I mean, that's good, I guess. Berto's told me more than once that being fetishized sounds fantastic—but trust me, it's not."

Her face softens, and I lower my hands.

"Yeah," she says. "I get that. You may not have noticed, but Maggie Ling and I are the only two women on Niflheim with epicanthal folds. I've gotten a little of that myself." She grins. "Tell you what. I won't objectify you if you won't objectify me."

I offer her my hand. "Done."

We shake. Her smile widens briefly, then fades when she drops my hand.

"Anyway," she says, "Gillian was part of the sortie yesterday."

"Oh," I say. "Right. *That* Gillian."

She nods, and looks away.

"Oh," I say. "Oh, I'm sorry. Afterward, you didn't seem . . . I mean . . ."

"I don't want to make this more than it is," she says. "She wasn't exactly my best friend. It's not the easiest thing, sharing a space that small with another person. If I'm being honest, most of the time we were barely friends at all."

"But still . . ."

"Yeah," she says. "But still. I went back to my rack after my shift ended today, and I just . . ."

"Couldn't?"

She rubs her face with both hands. "Right. I couldn't." She lets out a strangled laugh, then drops her face into her hands as it tails off into a sniffling sob. "You'd think I'd be psyched to have the place to myself, right?"

I reach out to touch her shoulder. She lifts her head to look at me, then scoots over until she's half onto my treadmill and our hips are touching. I slide my arm around her, and she leans her head against my chest.

"I'm sorry," she says. "You didn't come here to be my grief counselor." She straightens, and turns to look at me. "Why did you come here, really? You've got a solo rack, right? If you wanted privacy, why didn't you just go there?"

"That's a good question," I say.

She stares at me. I stare back. After what feels like forever but is actually probably more like ten seconds, she says, "Are you going to answer it?"

I sigh. "Nasha's there."

"Oh," she says. "Are you . . ."

"She's with someone else."

That stops her for a moment.

"In your rack," she says finally.

I shrug. She shakes her head.

"You know what? I don't want to know."

"Yeah," I say. "That's a good call."

We sit in silence then for a while. I'm starting to think that I'm going to have to go wander the corridors all night like the freaking phantom of Niflheim when she says, "I may regret this, but . . . I've got a double, you know."

I turn to look at her, one eyebrow raised. "Are you objectifying me right now?"

She laughs. "I am not. All I'm doing right now is offering an empty bed to a homeless person. I've gotta say, though—I'm kind of surprised that you and Nasha are open. Sure didn't seem like she thought so yesterday."

I shrug. "It's complicated."

"Okay," she says. "Is it the kind of complicated where I wind up getting gutted tomorrow?"

"No," I say. "I mean, probably not. Worst-case, I might get shoved down the corpse hole at some point."

She brings one finger to her chin and pantomimes deep thought.

"You know," she says finally, "I think that's a chance I'm willing to take."

"HEY," CAT SAYS. "Wake up."

I open my eyes. It takes me a disoriented minute to realize where I am. We pushed Cat's bed and her former roommate's together last night, but we both wound up sleeping on her side— Cat out of habit, I think, and me out of a vague sense that there's something disrespectful about crashing in a recently deceased person's bunk. Cat's propped up on one elbow now, with her arm pressing down on my shoulder and her face almost touching mine.

To be clear: nothing remotely sexual happened between us last night.

It may sound strange to hear that when I just said that we basically slept on top of one another, but when it came down to it I couldn't untangle what I was feeling about Cat from what I was feeling about Nasha and Eight, and Cat . . . I think she just needed a warm body to keep the monsters away.

I was okay with that. I know how she feels.

"It's almost nine," she says. "Do you need to be somewhere?"

That's actually a good question. I blink to the day's duty roster.

Looks like I'm supposed to be in Hydroponics today, trying to coax a bunch of half-dead vines to squeeze out a tomato or two. In fact, I was supposed to be there an hour ago. I haven't received a no-show, though, so Eight must be down there now, pinching off buds and checking pH levels.

Apparently I take duty on eaten-by-creepers days, and he takes duty when it's time to babysit plants. This is something we're going to need to discuss.

In the meantime, though, it looks like I've got a day to myself, for pretty much the first time since we made landfall. All I have to do is make sure I don't go anywhere near Eight, or bump into anyone else who might have seen him today.

This would be easier to accomplish if we didn't live in an inverted salad bowl less than a klick across.

"I'm off today," I say. "What about you?"

She shrugs. "I almost got killed in the line of duty twice in the past two days. In Security, I guess that earns you a half shift. I don't have to report until noon."

I wriggle out from under her arm and sit up, taking care not to jar my still-swollen left wrist any more than I have to. She rolls away and gets to her feet. We're both still wearing our underclothes, gray shapeless shirts and shorts covered in discolored patches from too much sweat and too many washings. They're so ugly that in a weird way seeing her like this feels almost more intimate than being naked.

"So?" Cat says. "What's your plan for the day?"

I rub my face with both hands and push my hair back from my forehead. She opens her locker and digs out a clean shirt.

"Not sure," I say. "It's been a while since I've had an off day."

The truth is that my plan is to slink around the dome hoping nobody sees me and realizes that I'm also down in Ag using an eyedropper to hand-feed baby tomatoes, but I can't really say that. Cat steps into her pants, then sits back down on the bed to pull on her boots.

"Well," she says, "my plan at the moment is to get something to eat. You interested?"

I grin. "Sure. You buying?"

She looks back over her shoulder with narrowed eyes. "No, I'm not buying," she says, "and just so you know, if you try touching my food again, you're gonna have two mangled hands instead of one."

Yeah, that's fair. I pull on my clothes, and we go.

THE HALLS ARE mostly empty at this time of day, and the few people we pass don't pay us much attention. Cat gets a few hellos, but even those folks mostly stare right through me. Especially since landfall, my job has been a pretty isolating one. For some reason, even most of the people who don't think I'm a soulless monster don't seem to want to associate with someone who's under what amounts to a perpetual death sentence.

At the moment, that seems to be working to my advantage.

Nobody wants to associate with someone who smells like a giant sweaty foot either, though, so we stop by the chem shower on the way down. Cat gives me an unreadable look when we get there. Is she asking if I want to share? I grin, give her a half bow, and wave her in. She shrugs, steps into the cubicle, and closes the door behind her. When she comes back out a few minutes later, I take my turn. I strip and scrub and dust-dry, and then climb back into my dirty clothes because even if I wanted to go back up to my rack, Eight is wearing my only clean change.

This reminds me that, while I miss a lot of things from Midgard to varying degrees, actual factual hot water is really close to the top of the list. The annoying thing is that there's clearly plenty of water lying around in drifts outside the dome. The systems *inside* the dome come straight from the *Drakkar,* though, so we still conserve water as if we're stuck in the interstellar desert. That won't change until we start doing local construction, and that won't happen unless and until a whole list of other things do, starting with metal fabrication and ending with resolving our issues with the creepers.

In the meantime, the chem shower is fine for sanitation, and it definitely keeps your body odor under control, but there's nothing remotely luxurious about it.

Not when you're in there by yourself, anyway.

That thought leads me to Nasha, and to Eight.

Best not to think about that now.

THE MAIN CAFETERIA is almost empty when we get there—just a couple at a table on the opposite side of the room from the food counter, heads close together, talking in whispers, and a lone Security goon near the entrance working his way through a pile of fried crickets. He nods to Cat as we pass him, and she gives him a finger-wave in return. I step to the counter and show my ocular to the scanner. It beeps, and my daily ration balance pops up in the upper left corner of my field of view.

It says I'm down six hundred kcal on the day. Looks like Eight had a big breakfast.

I'd like to be mad, but I can't blame him. The first couple days out of the tank really are a bitch.

I'm standing there, arms folded across my growling belly, trying to decide whether to splurge on a little mound of chopped yams to go with my mug of cycler paste and make this my only meal of the day, when Cat steps up beside me, close enough to brush against my shoulder.

"Are you going to order something?"

I scowl and tap the icon for the paste dispenser.

Cat smiles, shows her ocular, and orders a yam-tomato scramble. I can feel my mouth start to water, but that mound of yams I'd been eyeing might as well be a filet of beef given what's left on my balance. I grimace, gulp down a mouthful of paste from my mug, and then top it off before turning away. Three hundred kcal. That means I can have at least another half of a mug before bed tonight.

"I don't know how you stand that stuff," Cat says as her food slides out of a slot on the far side of the counter.

I glance over at her, open my mouth to say something rude, then think better of it and shake my head.

"If our friends in the Agriculture Section don't get their shit together soon," I say, "I think you're likely to find out."

She smirks. I pick up my mug of goo and take it to a table near the center of the room. Cat follows.

"You know," I say as she sits down, "you're kind of shoving your fancy-ass rich-person food in my face right now."

She laughs, but in a hesitant way that makes it clear that she's not entirely sure I'm kidding.

I am not, in fact, kidding.

None of my problems are her fault, though. I smile, and she visibly relaxes.

"Anyway," I say, "what's up in Security today? Anything new since that fiasco with the perimeter patrols?"

She takes a fat bite of her yams, chews, and swallows. I grimace and sip at my mug of paste.

"Well," she says around a second mouthful, "Amundsen is pretty worked up about this whole creeper issue. He's got us on a twelve-on-twelve-off duty cycle, which is a gigantic pain in the ass, and everyone who's on has to carry a linear accelerator at all times, which is also not great, because they're awkward and heavy and they leave you with sore shoulders at the end of a shift.

On the plus side, after what happened over the past two days, we're confined to the dome, so no more wandering around outside getting frostbite." She pauses to swallow. "I'm not even sure what he thinks we're supposed to do with an accelerator on the inside. Do you have any idea what kind of damage a ten-gram slug could do ricocheting around in here?"

She looks at me expectantly. It takes me a solid five seconds to realize that this wasn't a rhetorical question.

"Um," I say. "No?"

"A lot," she says. "That's what kind."

I'm most of the way through my paste by now. My belly still feels empty.

"Anyway," she says, "that's my jam. What about you? Have you had any more thoughts about how you're going to spend your day off?"

"Oh," I say, "you know. Hanging around. Sucking down cycler paste. Waiting to hear how Marshall's gonna kill me next. Just another day in paradise, I guess."

She laughs. Cat's laugh is not delicate. It's the sort of laugh you might expect to hear from someone who's just watched you slip on an ice patch.

"So tell me," she says as she scrapes up the last of her brunch, "what made you decide to get into the Expendable business?"

I think about making up some nonsense about service and duty, but for some reason I don't feel like I should be feeding self-serving lies to Cat. In the end I just shrug and tell her the truth.

"I wanted off of Midgard. This was the only way to make it happen."

"Ah," she says. "Got it."

I nod, turn up my mug, and let the last gritty dregs drain into my mouth.

"Wait," I say. "Got what? What do you got?"

"Why you signed on," Cat says. "You were a criminal, right? Killed somebody or something?"

This again.

"No," I say. "I didn't kill anyone."

"Huh. So what, then? Extortion? Armed robbery? Sex crimes?"

"No, no, and no. I'm not a criminal. If I were, do you really think they would have brought me onto Midgard's first colony mission?"

"As our Expendable? Yeah, maybe. During training I heard they were talking about conscripting someone."

"Yeah," I say. "I heard that too. Kinda raises questions about your judgment, doesn't it? You just let a murdering extortionist sex criminal spend the night in your room."

She grins. "I never said I was the brightest."

I run my finger around the inside of my mug to scrape up the bits of goo stuck to the bottom.

"Wow," Cat says. "You really like that stuff, huh?"

I scowl. "Oh yeah. It's the best."

She scrapes at her tray to get up the last burned bits of yam. "I never actually thought you were a murderer," she says. "I didn't believe they'd send someone like that on a colony mission, if only because they wouldn't want to screw up the gene pool. Most of the people I talked to, though, thought it was a lie when we heard that we'd gotten a volunteer. It's kind of hard to imagine someone just agreeing to . . . you know . . . do what you do. Gillian was sure you were a prisoner or something, and that they were feeding us a line about you volunteering so that we wouldn't ostracize you or whatever."

"Huh," I say. "That worked out great."

She rolls her eyes. "Oh come on. You've got friends. I've seen you around with Gomez, and Nasha seems to like you well enough. You still haven't answered my question, though. What were you thinking when you signed on to be the official crash test dummy for a beachhead colony?"

I could go into what actually got me into Gwen's office now.

I could, but I won't. Maybe a few self-serving lies wouldn't be so bad.

"Who knows?" I say. "Maybe I'm an idealist. Maybe I was just looking for a way to do my part for the Union."

She laughs again, harder this time. "Wow," she says. "How's that working out for you?" She sobers then, looks down at her empty tray and then back up at me. "Actually," she says, "it's working out pretty well for you, isn't it? Better than for Gillian or Rob or Dugan, anyway."

I'm not sure where she's going with this, but for some reason a chill runs down the back of my neck.

"What I mean," she says, "is that there are some definite advantages to being unkillable in a place like this, aren't there?"

"I'm not unkillable," I say. "I get killed all the damn time. That's the entire point of being an Expendable, isn't it?"

"And yet," she says, "here you are. Where's Gillian today?"

I don't have an answer for that. We sit in silence as Cat grimaces and downs a shot of cycler paste that she's gotten to supplement her meal. Medical says we all ought to be drinking a few hundred milliliters of paste per day for the vitamins. Apparently yams and crickets aren't actually a completely balanced diet. When she's done, Cat leans back in her chair and her smile returns.

"Anyway," she says, "totally unrelated, but I wanted to say . . . I guess . . . thanks, Mickey. I know last night was a little weird, but . . ."

"It wasn't weird," I say. "I get it."

She looks away. "Yeah. I just . . . I needed that, you know?"

I'm not sure what to say to that, so I reach across the table and touch her hand. She puts her other hand over mine for just a second before pulling away.

"Hey," she says, "what's your duty cycle look like tonight?"

I hesitate, but I can't come up with a good reason to lie about this. "I think I'm off tonight?"

She leans forward again, pushes back from the table, and picks up her tray. "Really? You're off now, right? How does that work?"

"You know," I say. "They make allowances when I'm fresh out of the tank."

"Wow," she says. "No kidding. The benefits just keep on coming, huh?"

I can't tell if she's smiling or not as she walks over to the refuse bin and drops her tray.

"Anyway," she says, "ping me around twenty-two hundred if you're free. Maybe we can do something fun together."

After Cat's gone, I dig out my tablet and run a search on the history of Expendables in colony expeditions. I'd always assumed that they were a standard part of the process, but in fact the technology has only been viable for the past two hundred years or so—and even in that span a lot of missions haven't made use of them. That seems crazy from a practical standpoint. When you're a half dozen lights from the nearest resupply, with a tiny pool of adults and a bunch of embryos that are going to take years of growing before they become useful, the ability to make new colonists more or less on demand ought to be compelling.

Turns out there are a lot of objections, though. The religious ones are obvious, even if they don't quite mesh with me. Apparently there are also some ethical issues with pulling someone off the streets or out of prison and forcing him to die for you over and over and over again. Landing a volunteer changes some of those considerations, obviously, but what are the odds of that happening?

It's possible I should have done some of this reading before giving Gwen my DNA. I'm not sure it would have dissuaded me—that torture machine was a powerful motivator—but I could at least have asked for a bigger signing bonus.

It's closing in on noon by the time I finish my reading, and the caf is starting to fill up. My stomach is already empty and rumbling, and watching my fellow colonists loading up their trays is not helping. I blink to my ration card. I've got four hundred and fifty kcal left for the day.

Correction. *We've* got four hundred and fifty kcal left for the day. If I'm going to stick to my deal with Eight, he's got a claim on three hundred of those.

That's a big if.

What's the worst that could happen if I went ahead and tanked our ration? It's not like Eight can go to Command with a complaint.

Of course, it's not like I can either. If I'd reported this mess two days ago, I probably would have been the one who didn't get disassembled. At this point, though, I'm confident that if Marshall gets wind of us, we're both in the slurry.

Also, Eight did say something this morning about murdering me in my sleep. I should probably just stick to the agreement.

That still leaves me with one-fifty to spend, but I can't imagine choking down another cup of slurry at the moment, so I decide to head back up to my rack and maybe take a nap to save energy.

On the central stairs, I have to edge past a man and a woman in Bio togs who are arguing about something in a loud, hand-flapping kind of way. I'm two steps past them when the man says, "Hey. Barnes?"

I turn, racking my brain for his name. Ryan? Bryan?

"Hey," I say. "What's up?"

"Not your shift," he says. "Where are you going?"

Uh-oh.

"I need to grab something from my rack," I say. "I'll be back down in five."

He scowls. "Make it three. We've got a new phage to test on the tomatoes this afternoon. It might be dangerous. They'll need you to help with the application."

"Sure," I say. "I'm on it."

They go back to arguing. I hesitate, then turn and continue, taking the stairs now two at a time.

After that, the whole nap thing turns out to be a bust. My heart is thudding in my chest by the time I get back to my rack, and it takes the better part of an hour for me to settle down enough to fall asleep. When I finally do, I wind up in the caterpillar dream again, but this time it's just a regular dream, and instead of talking he grows giant mandibles and feeding legs and starts chasing me through the forest. Pretty soon the forest fades and I'm back in the tunnels, running blindly, stumbling over loose stones while the skittering of a thousand tiny feet gets closer and closer behind.

I wake up to the sound of the door latch turning. It's Eight, back from his day playing farmer.

"Hey," I say once I've shaken off the nightmare and my heart has settled down into an almost-normal rhythm. "How are the tomatoes?"

He shakes his head. "Honestly? Not great. Most of the vines are dying, and the ones that aren't are squeezing out tomatoes that look more like overweight red raisins. Martin thinks there's something in the air—a microorganism, maybe, or some kind of trace gas—that's interfering with photosynthesis somehow. He doesn't have any actual candidates, though, so right now it's all speculation. The only thing we really know is that our tomatoes are sick." He pulls his shirt off over his head, then uses it to wipe a light sheen of sweat from his forehead. "Truth, though, it took everything I had not to shove the damn things into my mouth anyway."

"Yeah," I say. "I get that. Thanks for restraining yourself. If we wind up with another disciplinary ration cut, we're definitely going to starve to death."

He laughs, but there's no humor in it. "Pretty sure that's gonna happen anyway, friend-o. I used two-thirds of my ration this morning at breakfast, and I'm so hungry now that I could eat my own arm." He drops onto the bed. "Scoot over, huh?"

He pulls off his boots, and then lies back with a sigh.

"By the way," he says. "Have you been hanging around with Cat Chen?"

Uh-oh.

"Yeah," I say. "Sort of. Why?"

"Not sure. I ran into her on my way back up here, down near the main lock. She told me not to forget to ping her." He turns his head to look at me. "We're not screwing around on Nasha, are we? Because if we are, I have to tell you, I think that's a really, really bad idea."

"We are not," I say, and it's technically true. "Trust me—I'm just as interested in keeping all our pieces attached as you are."

"Good," he says. "Glad to hear it. Even putting Nasha aside, Chen seemed a little off, to be honest. She said something about my hand looking great, and she looked really confused when I said I didn't know what the hell she was talking about."

He glances down at my left hand lying across my belly. I've got it wrapped tight, but you can still see the purple bruise peeking out around the base of my thumb.

His wrap is slung across the back of our desk chair.

"Oh," he says. "Oh, right. That. Sorry."

SORRY.

Once again, thanks for that, asshole.

If you're not a member of the Natalist Church and you're not a student of Union history, you're probably wondering: Why am I so worked up about this? What's the big deal with multiples? I mean, on the surface, the idea of making a bunch of copies of your Expendable at once seems like a useful concept, doesn't it? For example, what happens if you've got a suicide mission that's a two-man job? Wouldn't want to risk an actual *person* for something like that, would you?

To understand the visceral reaction that most citizens have to the idea of multiples, you have to understand Alan Manikova, and you have to have at least a passing familiarity with what he did to Gault.

We've only had Expendables for a couple hundred years, but the bio-printer was actually invented long before that, even before the launch of the *Ching Shih*. Until Manikova came along, though, it wasn't much more than a curiosity. The systems they had then could scan a body, store the pattern, and re-create it down to the cellular level on demand, just like the bio-printer I pop out of every time Marshall gets me killed. Eventually they even figured out a way to reproduce synaptic connections, which modern systems don't bother doing. Theory at the time said that should be enough to accurately reproduce behavior if not consciousness, but repeated experiments, first with animals and later even with humans, demonstrated pretty clearly that their theory was fundamentally flawed. The things that came out of the bio-printers then were empty, tabula rasa bodies with less awareness or physical competence than a newborn baby. They were okay for creating fodder for medical experiments if you could overlook the obvious ethical issues, but they were not in any way a path to immortality.

To be fair, the old bio-printers weren't completely useless. People did occasionally use them to bring back babies who'd died in childbirth or shortly after—but even in those cases it usually didn't work out. The babies mostly came out of the tank breathing and with beating hearts, but they couldn't suck, couldn't swallow, couldn't cry. Sometimes, with a lot of intensive care, they made it through. More often, though, the parents just wound up burying another baby a few days or weeks after the first.

Then came Manikova.

Alan Manikova started life as the sole scion of a fantastically wealthy political dynasty on Eden. If he'd wanted to—and honestly, wouldn't you have wanted to?—he could have finished life that way as well. Most people in his position would have partied their way through school, maybe slipped into a mid-level government position at some point or maybe not, and either way spent their lives rich, fat, and happy.

Alan Manikova, though, wasn't most people. He was an epoch-defining genius, a mind so active and restless that he'd acquired doctorates in three seemingly unrelated fields before he turned twenty-five.

He was also a sociopath. That will become relevant later in the story.

Right around the time Manikova decided he was finished collecting graduate degrees, his parents both died suddenly, of unexplained causes, within a few days of one another. Six months later, after the local authorities had tried and failed to link Manikova to their deaths, he became one of the ten wealthiest people in the Union. Within a year, he'd plowed every penny of his inheritance into a venture he called Universal Eternity, Inc.

The popular press on Eden at the time thought that Universal Eternity was a boondoggle, or maybe some kind of tax dodge. Manikova didn't treat it that way, though. He could have kept the company virtual if the idea were to pull off some kind of financial scam, but he most definitely did not. Universal Eternity built a hulking research facility two hundred kilometers from the nearest town, hired huge numbers of engineers and scientists, and then . . .

Well, and then nothing. People came and went from the campus, but nobody said a word to anyone about what went on there. There was speculation that the company was engaged in aging research, or maybe in cryo-storage, but there was never any actual evidence for either theory. After a year or so, the press got bored, and people stopped paying attention to whatever Manikova was doing out there.

Five years later, he showed up on a talk show to announce that he'd finally uncovered the secret to recording and replicating a human mind.

Here again, we see the difference between Alan Manikova and most people. Immediately following an initial demonstration, in which he produced a duplicate of his company's HR director, had her say a few words to the assembled dignitaries, then immediately tranquilized her and broke her back down into slurry, the stock price of Universal Eternity skyrocketed, and Manikova went from being one of the ten richest people in the Union to far and away the richest, and in the public mind on Eden from a creepy possible parent killer to a creepy celebrity genius—maybe the greatest genius humanity had yet produced. Most people at this point would have acquired a palatial estate, maybe found a trophy spouse or two, and then spent the rest of their lives basking in the adulation.

Once again, Manikova didn't do any of that. Instead he liquidated everything he had, including Universal Eternity, Inc. The transactions involved so much cash and so many shell companies that he's one of the few people in history who can be credited with single-handedly causing a planetary economic recession. A year later, he boosted out of orbit alone in a custom-built interstellar transport packed with equipment, supplies, and the same prototype replication unit he'd used in his demonstration. He didn't tell anyone where he was going. Speculation was that he planned to become the first person to cross the galactic plane, reproducing himself as needed so that he'd still be alive at the end of the journey.

It would have been better for everyone if that had been the truth, but in fact he was bound for a recently established beachhead colony about seven lights anti-spinward from Eden that the founders had named Gault.

Even before Manikova showed up there, Gault was an interesting place. Unlike nearly every other successful colony in Union history, the expedition that founded it wasn't pulled together by Eden's planetary government. It was funded by a private group made up mostly of incredibly wealthy people who weren't happy with the fact that Eden, like Midgard and most other Union worlds, taxed the owners of the automated systems that produced pretty much everything in order to make sure that the people who didn't own those systems didn't starve in the streets.

The foundational principle on Gault was supposed to be Radical Liberty and Self Reliance, which in practice meant that none of the hundred and twenty colonists who made landfall there had the least interest in contributing anything whatsoever to the common good. They immediately broke into twenty-odd family groups, set up their own little fiefdoms, and tried to make do on their own. They'd all been pretty well resourced at the outset, and Gault was, all things considered, a pretty hospitable place, so most of them actually managed to establish themselves. The ones who had problems, though, didn't get any help from their neighbors. Apparently the Radical Liberty answer to, *Help, I'm dying*, is, *Well, you should have packed better*.

The upshot of all of this was that when Manikova arrived, he found a fragmented society of about ten thousand people, most of whom were reasonably well settled and not in immediate danger of starving to death, but none of whom were doing particularly well. At first he was greeted as a bit of a savior. He'd brought a lot of stuff with him, stuff that none of the individual groups on Gault had yet gotten around to being able to produce for themselves. He ingratiated himself with one of the smaller clans, gave them food and seeds and some shiny new tech that had been developed on Eden in the two hundred years or so since they'd boosted out. They gave him a place to live and a base of operations.

Once he was safely established, he set himself single-mindedly to making more Alan Manikovas.

As Marshall has emphasized to me more than once, building a human being from scratch takes a lot of resources. In particular, you need a lot of calcium and a lot of protein, but there are a bunch of other things that go into the mix as well. You can feed the hopper of a bio-printer with basic elements, but it takes a huge pile of wheat and beef and oranges to get everything you need for the job, and the process produces an ungodly amount of waste if you're not interested in churning the leftovers into food for a starving colony.

The ideal source of raw materials, obviously, is an already-existing human body.

It took Manikova about nine months to run through the supply of feedstock he'd brought with him to Gault. By that time he had close to a hundred copies of himself running around, and had built two additional replication units. It was another few months after that before anyone noticed that people were going missing. He'd begun the project by snatching up indigents and loners, of which Gault, by its nature, had a ton, but eventually he ran out of those and had to start grabbing people who had family and friends to miss them. Suspicion, as it always does, fell immediately on the new guy in town. The clan that had been hosting him sent Security forces to his compound to bring him in for some polite questioning.

This is when they learned that, while Manikova had been generous with seeds and trinkets, he hadn't shared the advanced military tech that he'd brought along.

On a more reasonable world—not even one with a single unified government, necessarily, but maybe one where the different polities at least talked to one another occasionally—Manikova might have been stopped. When it became apparent what he was up to, he was still outnumbered on the planet by a factor of twenty-to-one. Gault, unfortunately, was not a reasonable world. Manikova shoved every citizen of his host clan into the hopper, cranked them back out as copies of himself, armed them, and then launched an assault on his nearest neighbor. It was nearly a year before the surviving clans even considered mounting a unified response to him. By then, Manikova was an absolute majority of the humans on the planet. The last few clans did eventually pull together, but it was much too late by then. The only useful thing they really accomplished was to get a last, desperate message back to Eden, describing what had happened to them and begging for help from the home world.

Help wasn't coming anytime soon, of course. It took seven years for their message to reach Eden, and once it did, it took the authorities there almost two years to decide what, if anything, to do about it. The folks who had left to found Gault had not been particularly well thought-of on Eden when they boosted out, and the ensuing years hadn't improved their reputation. Public sentiment tended pretty heavily toward *not our problem* and *serves them right*. In the end, though, Eden's parliament decided that Manikova might at some point actually pose a threat to other worlds, and so would need to be dealt with.

This was the origin of the Union's first, and so far only, interstellar military expedition.

A lot of thought went into what, exactly, an invasion across seven light-years ought to look like. The idea of ground forces was obviously absurd. Eden was an immensely rich world, but its budget would be stretched close to breaking just putting together and fueling something similar to a colony ship. They didn't need to worry about carrying terraforming equipment or fetuses, obviously, but military equipment is heavy too. In the end, they settled on a slightly up-armored colony ship that they called *Eden's Justice*. It boosted out of Eden's system four years after Gault's message arrived, carrying a crew of two hundred, a half dozen orbital bombardment craft, and an enormous number of fusion bombs. The thought was that they would settle into orbit around Gault, make contact with Manikova, determine what his intentions were *vis-à-vis* the rest of the Union in general and Eden in particular, and then, if necessary, glass the planet over.

You're probably already seeing the flaws here.

First, by the time they got to Gault, Manikova had had almost eighteen years to consolidate his hold on the system, create ever more copies of himself, and dig himself in.

Second, stealth was simply not an option for *Eden's Justice*. A starship's deceleration torch is visible from a light-year out, and there's not really a way to disguise it.

Third, and probably most importantly, Alan Manikova was not the sort of person who was inclined to wait for the fight to come to him.

The upshot of all this was that the Battle of Gault lasted something on the order of twelve seconds. *Eden's Justice* was still decelerating, blinded by her own torch to what was coming, when a dozen or so nuclear-tipped missiles slammed into her from a base Manikova had built on Gault's second moon. Her commander never even managed to get off a retaliatory shot.

Unfortunately for Alan Manikova, but probably fortunately for the rest of the Union, Eden wasn't the only world that had received Gault's last messages. They were also picked up by Gault's next-closest neighbor, a much younger, poorer, second-gen colony called Farhome. The government there was, if anything, more alarmed than the one on Eden. They didn't have either the ambition or the resources to mount the sort of expedition that Eden had attempted, though.

Their response was much simpler, more direct, and much, much cheaper. They called it *The Bullet*.

The critical thing about interstellar travel is this: kinetic energy is equal to the mass of an object times its velocity squared. That makes the process very expensive. It also makes it very dangerous. *Eden's Justice* was betrayed by her deceleration torch. *The*

Bullet avoided that problem by never attempting to decelerate. When an object is moving at 0.97 *c*, as *The Bullet* was when it slammed into Gault three months after the destruction of *Eden's Justice,* it doesn't have to be all that massive in order to crack a planet open like an eggshell. Even better, there's no practical way to defend against a relativistic attack, or even really to know that it's coming, because the light waves announcing its arrival reach its target a bare fraction of a second before it does. *The Bullet* delivered the energy equivalent of two hundred thousand fusion bombs to Gault's ecosystem over a period of roughly a picosecond.

You just don't come back from something like that.

As the fact that we're trying to make it work on Niflheim shows—there just aren't a lot of habitable planets hanging around waiting for us out here. Turning one of them into a ball of molten slag is widely considered to be the single greatest crime in the history of the Union.

Nobody blames Farhome for it, though. They blame Manikova— and ever since, in most parts of the Union you're better off in most people's minds being a child stealer or a human head collector than you are being a multiple.

Twenty-two Hundred comes. I don't ping Cat. Does she know for sure what's going on with me and Eight? Maybe not, but after her run-in with him this afternoon she definitely knows something's up, and somehow I don't think she's the sort of person to just let abominations slide. I'm starting to feel like my best chance at not getting converted into protein paste at this point is to avoid her for as long as possible, and hope that she gets eaten by creepers in the meantime.

That plan doesn't last long. Cat pings me at 22:02:

<CChen0197>: So. You free?

"So much for staying out of her way," Eight says. "You gonna answer?"

I turn to look at him. He's stretched out on the bed with his hands folded behind his head. I'm in the swivel chair, feet propped up on the desk. I'd been reading about yet another colonial disaster—this one a beachhead that died of insurrection and civil war before it even had a chance to earn a real name—but the

narrative wasn't really grabbing me. Mostly, I've been perseverating on the idea of getting shoved down the corpse hole.

"Yeah," I say. "I guess I have to, don't I?"

<Mickey8>:Hey Cat. I was just catching up on some stuff, but yeah,
    I'm free.

The more often I see myself tagged as Mickey8, the weirder it
feels. I imagine the foreboding that eight at the end of my name
calls down on me right now is kind of like what a regular person
might feel if she walked past a grave marker with her name on it.

<CChen0197>:Great. We should talk.
<Mickey8>:Meet at your rack?
<CChen0197>:...
<CChen0197>:I don't think so, Mickey. Let's go with the gym again,
    huh? Meet me there in ten.
<Mickey8>:Uh ... sure. See you then.

"The gym?" Eight says. "What's up with that?"

I shrug.

"Seriously," he says. "Who works out during a famine?"

"It's a thing," I say. "I ran into her there last night, when I
was afraid to come back here because I thought you might have
Nasha with you."

"I did, just FYI."

I shoot him a glare. He crosses his legs at the ankle and grins.

"Anyway," he says, "be careful. There's something off about her."

"Whatever," I say. "If she murders me, you get to go to full
rations, right?"

His grin widens. "Good point. Hey—what are you gonna do
about that hand?"

I look down. The swelling is mostly gone, but I've still got it wrapped.

"Dunno," I say. "I could take off the bandage, I guess?"

"I wouldn't. It's still purple. Just . . . I don't know . . . keep your hand in your pocket?"

I shake my head. "I don't think so. Honestly, it hurts just thinking about doing that. Maybe you should go instead of me?"

"No," he says. "No chance. You two have a history. What if she wants to talk about whatever went down between the two of you last night?"

Unfortunately, that's a fair point.

"Anyway," he says, "I actually worked today, and I'm tired. Have a fun time."

He closes his eyes. I open my mouth to reply, but I've got nothing. I get to my feet, and I go.

I'm halfway to the gym when my ocular pings.

<Mickey8>:Ar chi** ?

What the hell?

<Mickey8>:Eight?
<Mickey8>:What?
<Mickey8>:Co m . . . ren?
<Mickey8>:What the hell, Seven?
<Mickey8>:Go back to sleep, Eight. I don't have time for this.
<Mickey8>:Mol**an inv?

Whatever. I cut the connection.

"Hey," Cat says. "Why didn't you ping me?"

She's sitting on one of the treadmills. She doesn't look like she's dressed to run this time.

"I was going to," I say. "You didn't give me a lot of slack."

She shrugs. "Doesn't matter. It's fine. Have a seat."

She pats the other treadmill. I hesitate, then decide that if she plans to kill me, she doesn't need to trick me into sitting on a treadmill to do it. I sit.

"So," I say. "Um . . . are we working out?"

She stares at me for what feels like a long while.

"No," she says finally. "We are not working out. We're in the gym because I wanted to speak with you privately, and this is the last place that anyone in this colony other than me would come voluntarily."

"We could have met in your room."

She looks away. "I don't think that's a good idea. Not until we get some things sorted out, anyway. Clear?"

"Yeah," I say. "Clear. So. What are we talking about?"

She gives me another long look. "How's your hand, Mickey?"

I sigh. "Getting better. Thanks for asking."

She nods. "It was all the way better this afternoon."

No point in dragging this out. "Look," I say. "Tell me what we're here for."

"Okay," she says. "Cards on the table. There's two of you, Mickey. You're the one I had breakfast with this morning. You're the one who was in my bed last night. You've got a busted hand, and you were off shift today. The other one, who I ran into in the corridor a few hours ago, has an unbusted hand, and spent the day growing tomatoes. I don't know how or why, but you're a multiple."

And I knew she knew this, but still my stomach knots, and I can suddenly feel my heart pounding in my throat. "Have you talked to Command?"

She manages to look offended. "Seriously? You sort of saved

my life two days ago, and yesterday I saved yours. *You slept in my bed.* After all that, do you really think I'd just turn you in without talking first?"

I close my eyes, and the clench in my belly relaxes slightly.

"Don't get me wrong," she says. "I definitely have a serious problem with what you're doing. How the hell did you get Bio to make you a multiple, anyway? That's a capital offense for everyone involved, isn't it?"

I shake my head. "I didn't *get* them to make me a multiple. I know what the law says, and I don't have any interest in getting turned into slurry. It was a mistake."

She raises one eyebrow. "A mistake? Like somebody tripped and fell on the bio-printer, and you came squirting out the other end?"

"Sure," I say. "Something like that."

She opens her mouth, hesitates, then shakes her head. "You know what? I don't want to know. If the shit winds up coming down on you, I don't want to be implicated. That's the other reason I didn't want you in my room. I'll tell you, though—it won't be long before somebody who *does* want to know is going to figure out that something is up with you, and when they do, you'll want to have a better story ready than, 'It was a mistake.' "

"Yeah," I say. "You're probably right."

We sit in silence for a while. I'd like to ask her what she brought me here for. It doesn't look like she wants to kill me, and she hasn't indicated anything about blackmail yet. My only other guess was that she wanted to pick up where we left off this morning, but "I definitely have a serious problem with what you're doing" seemed to rule that one out. I'm thinking about wishing her a good evening and heading back up to my rack when she says, "Do you think you're immortal?"

Did not expect that.

"What?"

"Do you think you're immortal? You've been killed, what, seven times?"

"Six," I say. "It's only six so far. That's kind of the root of the problem."

"Whatever. Are you the same person you were when you boarded the shuttle off of Midgard?"

I have to think about that.

"Well," I say finally. "This isn't the same body, obviously."

"Right," Cat says. "That's not what I was asking."

"Yeah," I say, "I know. So, yeah, I remember being Mickey Barnes back on Midgard. I remember the apartment he grew up in. I remember his first kiss. I remember the last time he saw his mother. I remember signing on for this stupid expedition. I remember all of that stuff as if it was me who did it, not someone else. Does that mean I *am* Mickey Barnes, though?" I shrug. "Who the hell knows?"

She's staring at me. Her eyes are narrowed, and I feel that chill from this morning running down the back of my neck again.

"I looked up that Ship of Theseus thing. You did a terrible job describing it."

"Yeah," I say. "I know. That's one of those things that I thought I remembered from training, but then when I started talking I realized that, no, I didn't actually remember it at all."

"I'm surprised. It's a pretty tight analogy for your life. I'd think it would have stuck with you."

I shrug. "Sorry."

"It's a pretty airtight argument, don't you think?"

I start to answer, then shake my head and start again. "I'm confused, Cat. Where are you going with this?"

"Where I'm going is, I want to know if you're Mickey Barnes, or if you're just some other guy running around in his clothes."

"I told you," I say, "I don't know. I know what Jemma told me back on Himmel Station, and I know that I *feel* like I'm the same person I was back on Midgard, but . . . I don't know. That's the flip side of the argument, isn't it? The fact that it doesn't make any measurable difference in any way whether I'm the same person or I'm not means that there's no possible way for me to know for sure. It's an unanswerable question."

"Still," she says, "you don't know that you're *not* him, right?"

"No," I say. "I guess I don't."

She doesn't respond. We sit in silence for a while. I'm about to ask if we're done here when she says, "You know, I've been thinking a lot these past two days."

"Um," I say. "Okay. What about?"

"Dying. I've been thinking about dying. I'm only thirty-four years old. I shouldn't have to think about dying for another fifty years, but here we are."

Beachhead colonies are dangerous places. I wonder if they emphasized that as heavily in her training as they did in mine. I don't get a chance to ask, though, because apparently she's heard all that she needed to hear. She gets to her feet, and then offers me a hand up.

"Look," she says. "I like you, Mickey."

"Thanks," I say. "I like you too."

"You're a good guy, I think. If it weren't for this whole multiple thing . . ."

If it weren't for that, I would have been with Nasha last night instead of with her, but this probably isn't the time to say that. I'm standing there trying to come up with something that I *can* say when she rises up onto her toes and kisses my cheek. She steps back, gives me a sad smile, and opens the door.

"Tell the other you I said hello, huh?"

I stand staring, my jaw hanging slightly open, as she walks away.

* * *

THE DOOR TO my room is locked when I get there. I show my ocular, wait for the click of the latch disengaging, and then push it open. It's dark inside, but in the wash of light from the corridor I can see that there are two people lying on my bed.

Two naked people.

One of them is Eight. The other is Nasha.

I stand there, frozen. I have no idea what I'm supposed to be feeling right now. Jealousy? Anger?

Abject terror?

"Get in here," Eight says. "Close the door."

"But you're . . ." I sputter. "What the shit, Eight? What the actual shit?"

"Sorry," he says. "I thought you'd be spending the night with Chen again. That or be dead, anyway."

Nasha rises up on one elbow. "You slept with somebody else?"

"No," I say. "I mean, yes, I slept in her room, but we didn't . . ."

"Oh," she says. "You just cuddled?"

I open my mouth to protest before realizing that she's laughing at me.

"I'm sorry," I say. "You were with Eight."

"Eight?" Nasha says. "Is that what you're calling each other now? Seven and Eight?"

"Yeah," Eight says. "Got a better suggestion?"

"No," she says. "It's kind of cute, I guess."

"Eight," I say.

"Seven," he says. "Close the door."

I do. It's dark enough now that my ocular flips over to infrared. Eight shows up as dull orange. Nasha is bright, glowing red. I drop into the desk chair and lower my head into my hands.

"So," Eight says. "How'd it go with Chen, anyway?"

I look up at him. "What? Who cares about Chen? What are you doing here, Eight?"

"Seriously?" Eight says. "I thought that was pretty obvious."

"No!" I say. "What I mean is . . . fuck you! You know exactly what I mean!"

"What Eight is doing," Nasha says, her voice a low, feline rumble, "is stealing away your woman. What're you gonna do about it?"

"Eight," I say, "we talked about this. Why didn't you ask me before you brought Nasha into this?"

"Oh, relax," Nasha says. "I'm not about to turn you two pervs in to Command."

"We're not pervs," I say. "It was an accident."

"I told her what happened," Eight says. "She's just screwing with you. Seriously, though—what happened with Chen? Did she try to kill you?"

"Chen?" Nasha says. "Cat Chen, from Security?"

"Yeah," I say. "You said yesterday that you were gonna gut her like a fish, remember?"

"Only if she touched you. Did she touch you, Mickey?"

"No," I say. "I mean, yeah, sort of, but she's not interested in that, I don't think—especially not now. She seemed pretty put off by the whole multiple thing."

"Not surprised," Nasha says. "Security types all have rods up their asses."

"Back up," Eight says. "She knows?"

"Yeah," I say. "She knows. The whole miraculously healing and unhealing hand tipped her off. Also, you apparently told her you'd been in the Agriculture Section today, while I told her today was an off-shift."

"Huh," Eight says. "That's not good. How'd you leave it?"

I sigh. "Honestly, I have no idea. She didn't say she was turning us in, so I guess that's good. She didn't exactly say she wasn't either, though, so I guess that's not so great."

"Did you think about gutting her?" Nasha asks. "Leave her outside the main lock, say a creeper got her? Problem solved, right?"

Eight snickers. "If anybody was getting gutted tonight, it wasn't gonna be Chen."

"Truth," I say. "Not sure what you're giggling about, though. If I go down the corpse hole, you're going with me, remember?"

"Nobody's going down the corpse hole," Nasha says. "Chen won't turn you in."

"Really?" I say. "Why not?"

I mean, I don't think so either, but I'm assuming Nasha's reasons for thinking that are very different from mine.

"Because," she says, "she doesn't want to deal with the blowback."

"Blowback?" Eight says.

"Me," Nasha says. "I'm the blowback."

She makes a good point, actually. I wouldn't cross her.

Of course, I wouldn't cross Cat either. Security goons are spooky.

"Look," Nasha says, "everything's gonna be fine. You two just need to lie low until one or the other of you gets offed doing some dumbass suicidal thing. Then we can register whichever one of you is still alive as Mickey9, and everybody lives happily ever after."

"Well," Eight says. "Almost everybody."

"Right," Nasha says. "Almost."

"I don't know," I say. "It's only been a couple of days since Eight came out of the tank, and we've already got two other people who know about us. At this rate, the entire colony will be in on this in a couple of weeks. I'm not sure I can die that fast."

Nasha laughs. "You know what, Mickey? You think too much. Take off those clothes and get in here. You need to shift some blood away from your brain for a while."

I stare at her. "Come on, Seven," Eight says. "We're already perverts, right? And blowback or not, I'm not too confident that we're not both going down the corpse hole soon enough. Might as well have some fun while we're here."

THE NEXT TWO hours are weird. I don't think I want to talk about them.

Just to be clear, though: I regret nothing.

THE THREE OF us are just settling into that soft, calm after-place, with me hanging off one side of the bed, Eight on the other, and Nasha pressed in between us, when someone knocks on the door. Nasha had been saying something to Eight about how much fun we were going to have until one of us got recycled, but she cuts off midsentence with a hiss of indrawn breath.

The knock comes again.

"Should I answer?" I whisper. "I could try to get rid of them."

Eight reaches across Nasha to slap the side of my head. "Shut up," he hisses. "That's probably Berto. If we're quiet, he'll go away."

"Mickey? Are you in there?"

Oh shit. That's not Berto.

Nasha shifts around until her mouth is next to my ear.

"You did set the security lock, right?"

The latch disengages with a quiet *snick,* and a crack of light appears around the door.

"No," I whisper. "I did not."

"Mickey?"

Fuck. Fuck fuck fuck.

The door swings open.

"Hey," Eight says. "Chen, right? Good to see you."

Cat stares at us, her mouth working silently.

"Cat?" I say. "Close the door. We can talk about this."

She shakes her head.

"Cat?"

I sit up and reach out to her. She takes a half step back. "What are you doing, Mickey?"

"What does it look like?" Nasha says. "Get in or get out, Chen. Either way, close the door."

Cat turns on her heel and bolts, leaving the door standing open behind her.

"You probably want to close that," Nasha says.

I climb out of bed and swing the door shut. This time, I remember to set the privacy lock.

"This is bad," I say, and slump down into the desk chair.

"She already knew about us," Eight says. "You said that, right? So, nothing's changed."

That almost makes sense. So why is my heart trying to beat its way out of my chest?

"It's fine," Nasha says. "Come back to bed, Mickey."

I take a deep breath, hold it, and then let it out again. Maybe they're right?

They're not right. I know they're not.

Nothing to do about it now, though. I pull back the sheet, and climb back into bed. Nasha twists around to kiss me.

"Relax, Mickey. Let's get some sleep."

I WAKE IN the darkness to the *snick* of the privacy lock being overridden. After that comes a rush of light, and then a deep male voice saying, "You've got to be kidding me." I squint into the glare coming in from the corridor. Two Security goons have wedged themselves into my room. They're both carrying burners.

"Holy shit," the smaller one says. "What the hell is wrong with you people?"

The other shakes his head. "Doesn't matter. Get up, all three of you, and for shit's sake put some clothes on. You've all got a date with the cycler."

I'M LOSING IT.

The fact that I'm losing it makes me feel even worse than the actual losing it does.

Nasha has every right to be freaking out right now. She's never been marched off to her own execution before. I've got no excuse, though. This is practically routine for me. I once had three executions in two weeks.

A COLONY SHIP doesn't just land when it reaches its destination. Most of what gets us from one star to another is built strictly for space. It's too bulky and too fragile to survive entering an atmosphere or exposing itself to a gravitational field. A colony comes down from orbit in bits and pieces.

The first bit to come down to the surface of Niflheim, just a few hours after we made orbit, was a lander piloted by Nasha containing a biological isolation chamber, a team from Medical, a team from Biology, and me.

We already knew by then that we were more or less boned when it came to both the climate and the atmospheric composition of our new home. Marshall had actually considered trying to push on to a secondary target when he realized that we wouldn't be able to survive outside without rebreathers, but after a lot of discussion and a fair bit of yelling, Dugan and a few others from Bio convinced him that once we'd introduced some engineered algae into the ecosystem, we'd be able to get the partial pressure of oxygen in the atmosphere up to survivable levels within a reasonable time frame—reasonable in this case meaning not necessarily within the lifetimes of any of the adult members of the expedition, but possibly within the lifetimes of some of the embryos we were carrying in the hold.

As I think I mentioned, the odds of an expedition like ours ever reaching a secondary target are not-quite-but-almost zero, so in the end he decided to give Niflheim a go.

The first order of business for any new colony is determining whether there's anything in the local microbiota that might pose a hazard to human health.

For the record, there is always something in the local microbiota that not only might, but in fact definitely will, pose a hazard to human health.

The way this is determined, naturally, is by exposing the expedition's Expendable to anything and everything that can be isolated from the local environment, and then waiting to see what happens to him.

We'd been on the surface for less than a day when Nasha gave me a last kiss and a pat on the cheek, and then a tech from Medical named Arkady marched me into the isolation chamber. The last thing he did before he left me there was fit me with a scanning helmet for continuous upload. When I asked him what that was for, he said, "I guess they might want to ask you what you thought about this later."

"Seriously?" I said. "You're gonna give me super-herpes? Fine. That's my job. Do I really have to remember it?"

He shrugged, backed out of the chamber, and closed the door.

THE ISOLATION CHAMBER was a cylinder just wide enough that I could almost touch both sides if I stretched out my arms, and just tall enough that I could stand up without hitting my head. It had a metal chair in the center that doubled as a toilet if you slid back a lid on the seat, a vent in the ceiling, and a drawer set into the wall opposite the door where they'd left me some snacks, in case I didn't die right away. I'd just sat down when the vent began hissing.

"Take a few deep breaths," Arkady said through the intercom. "Breathe through your mouth, if you don't mind."

I actually didn't, because whatever was coming out of the vent smelled like dog farts.

It tasted like dog farts too.

After a minute or so of that, the vent closed with an audible click.

"Thanks," Arkady said. "Make yourself comfortable. This may take a while."

I had to bite back the urge to tell him that I hated to inconvenience him, and that I'd try to die as quickly as possible.

A few minutes after that, Nasha's face appeared in the door's tiny window.

"Hey," she said. "How's it going in there?"

I grimaced. "Great." I gestured to the drawer behind me. "They gave me snacks."

She smiled. "Lucky you. All we've got out here is cycler paste and water."

I turned around and rooted through the drawer, found a protein bar, and peeled off the wrapper.

"Well," I said, and took a bite. "Nothing but the best for the sacrificial pig, right?"

"Lamb," she said.

"What?"

"Lamb, Mickey. You sacrifice a lamb. Pigs are gross. You don't sacrifice them. You just eat them."

I sighed. "Either way, they end up just as dead."

NASHA TRIED. HONEST to God, she did. She'd probably known since we first kissed that someday she'd have to watch me die, but after eight years it was finally happening, and I don't think she knew what to do. I don't think she knew what to *feel*. So she stood outside that window for four hours, and she talked to me. She talked about what the planet looked like through the viewscreens. She talked about what a jackass Arkady was. She talked about some vid drama she'd been watching about a family of obscenely wealthy assholes on Midgard.

She talked about the stuff we could do together when this was over, when I came back out of the tank again.

I tried too, because she was trying, and I didn't want her to feel any worse than she probably already did. After a couple of hours, though, I wasn't feeling so well myself. At first I thought it must be psychosomatic. Who ever heard of a bug starting in on you that quickly, right? Before long, though, it was pretty clear that I was spiking a fever. Arkady came back to ask me a few questions about what I was feeling. I told him it felt like the early stages of the flu. He nodded and went away again. The coughing started at three hours. I first brought up blood at three and a half. Nasha had mostly stopped talking by then, but she was still there, watching me through the window, one hand pressed against the glass next to her face.

At the four-hour mark, I mustered up enough breath to tell her to go away. I didn't want her watching what came next.

She didn't go away. When it was clear what was happening, she arm-twisted Arkady into strapping her into a biohazard suit so that she could come into the chamber with me. I didn't want her there at first. When things got really bad, though, when I started coughing so hard that I cracked a rib and brought up chunks of tissue, she held my hand and cradled my head against her belly and talked me through it. It was awful, what she did then, and it was beautiful, and if I live another thousand years I will never stop being grateful for it.

It was only another hour or so after that. Just for future reference: If you have any choice in the way you leave this life, try to stay away from pulmonary hemorrhage. I think I can speak from a position of authority on this topic. This is not the way you want to go.

I WOKE UP naked and covered in goo, laid out on the floor next to the portable tank they'd brought down in the lander.

"Really?" I said when I'd coughed the last of the fluid out of my no longer bleeding lungs. "I don't even get a bunk?"

Burke, my friend from Medical, tossed me a towel. "You were covered in crap," he said. "I didn't want to wash the bedding."

I scraped as much gunk off of myself as I could, then climbed into the one-piece gray coverall he handed me.

"Get something to eat," he said. "You've got at least twenty-four hours before you go back in."

"So," NASHA SAID. "That was rough."

I looked at her across the common room table. She wouldn't meet my eyes.

"Yeah," I said. "That was rough. Thanks for staying with me."

She looked up at the ceiling, then down at her hands—anywhere but at me.

"Mickey . . ." she said.

I waited for her to go on, but when it was pretty clear she couldn't, I let her off the hook.

"You don't have to do it again," I said. "Nobody should have to watch someone they . . ."

"Love," she said.

In spite of myself, I smiled. We'd been together for eight years by then, but that was the first time either one of us had said that word.

"You shouldn't have to watch me die more than once."

"No," she said. "I'll be there. Dying . . . even if it's temporary, you shouldn't have to do it with nobody around for company but that little bitch Arkady."

I reached across the table. Our fingers intertwined.

"Anyway," she said, "somebody's got to be there to make sure you don't sneak away."

As it happened, it was almost a week before they sent me back into the chamber. I spent most of that time with Nasha. We talked sometimes, we played a few rounds of a card game she'd brought down from the *Drakkar*. Mostly, though, we held each other. There wasn't much else to do.

After four days, Burke came into the tiny, curtained-off nook where I'd been sleeping, had me pull up my sleeve, and gave me a half dozen injections with needles that looked like sawed-off water pipes. Halfway through he had to switch arms because my left shoulder was already turning purple. When I asked him what they were, he gave me a look that said clearly that he didn't think he should have to explain himself to the guinea pig. When

I asked again, though, he rolled his eyes and said, "The first two were immune boosters. The other four were vaccines against the microorganisms that killed your last iteration. We'll give it two days for them to take effect, and then try again."

"Great," I said. "So you think I've got a chance this time?"

He looked at me, then shrugged and turned away. "You never know," he said, then added after he'd let the curtain swing back behind him, ". . . but probably not."

I DON'T REMEMBER what happened to Mickey4. I know that he died in Nasha's arms, more or less just like Mickey3, because they made me watch the surveillance video later. I don't remember it, though, because the first thing he did when they opened the vents in the isolation chamber was to unplug the leads from the scanning helmet and take it off.

"Hey," Arkady said. "What the hell are you doing?"

He rolled his eyes. "What does it look like?"

"You need to put that back on," Arkady said. "You're breaking protocol."

Four shook his head. "Sorry, Arkady. If the inoculations work, we can do a full recording as soon as you let me out of here. If they don't . . ."

"If they don't, we'll be losing valuable data."

He rolled his eyes. "Valuable data? What the hell are you talking about? You didn't ask me a single question about what happened to Three."

"We know what happened to your last iteration, Barnes. He bled out through the lungs. We didn't need to ask any questions about that. What if what happens to you is more interesting?"

Four stared at him through that little window for a solid ten seconds, then burst out laughing.

"Interesting?" he said when he'd finished. "Interesting? I'll tell you what, asshole. If anything *interesting* happens to me while I'm in here, I'll be sure to let you know. Fair enough?"

"Barnes," Arkady said. "Put the helmet on. Now."

Four folded his arms across his chest and smirked out at him.

"Those biohazard suits are fragile," he said. "It'd be pretty easy to knock a hole in one of them, wouldn't it? Give that some thought, and then come in here and make me."

AS IT TURNED out, what happened to Four was not particularly interesting. He lasted a lot longer than Three did—over twenty-four hours before he started showing any symptoms. When the bug that killed him got going, though, it worked quickly. It cleared out his GI tract first, with fluid pouring out of both ends in great, bloody torrents. When there wasn't anything more to be done on that front, it went to work on his liver and his kidneys. He was septic at thirty-two hours, and unconscious at thirty-six. By hour forty, he was dead.

I WOKE UP on the floor again. This time, there were eleven needles waiting for me.

"Wow," I said. "That was quick."

"Not really," said Burke. "It's been eight days since the last trial. Dugan told us not to bring you back this time until we were ready with the next round of inoculations. No point in wasting resources feeding you when you're just going back in the hopper anyway, right?"

He worked his way through the injections. Four in the right shoulder, three in the left, and the rest in my right thigh.

"Oh," he said when he was done. "Dugan also said to tell you that Marshall says you're wearing the helmet this time."

"No," I said. "I'm not."

"Yeah," he said. "He thought you'd say that. He also said to tell you that if you don't, we're authorized to throw your next iteration into the chamber without any shots, and to keep doing that as many times as we need to until you get with the program."

He walked away then, and left me sitting naked on the edge of the tank to ponder which is worse: an infinite loop of torment that you don't remember a bit of, or a single bad death that's stuck in your head forever.

IN THE END, I put on the helmet. Nasha came to see me off again. This time, when she kissed me, she wrapped her arms around me and didn't let go until Arkady pulled her away.

"This is the one," she said as I stepped into the chamber. "You're coming back out this time."

"What do you think?" I asked Arkady as he was hooking up the leads to the helmet. "Is this the one?"

He shrugged. "Stranger things have happened."

AFTER A DAY in the chamber, I felt fine.

AFTER TWO DAYS, I felt fine.

AFTER THREE DAYS, I was cranky and stiff from trying to sleep in that stupid chair, and my snack drawer was running low. Otherwise, though, I felt fine.

ON THE MORNING of the eighth day, Arkady told me to strip naked, stand spread-eagled, hold my breath, and close my eyes. For the next thirty seconds, I was doused in a series of increasingly caustic and almost definitely toxic sprays.

"Breathe," Arkady said when that was done, "but keep your eyes closed."

Even through my tight-clenched eyelids, the glare of the UV disinfectant was painful.

That cycle repeated three times.

By the time it was done, I was bloodred from head to toe and felt like I'd been flayed alive.

But I was alive.

For the first time, I walked back out of the isolation chamber.

"Get dressed," Arkady said, "and get down to Medical. You're not out of the woods yet, friend."

"Hey," Nasha said. "Can I go with?"

Arkady looked at her for a long moment, then shook his head. "Best not. If he checks out there, you can have at him. Until then, he's still a potential vector."

My exam was almost perfect.

Almost.

Blood work, physical exam, skin cultures, throat cultures, sinus cultures—everything came out clean. The last thing they did was a whole-body magnetic resonance scan.

"Just to be sure," Burke said.

Famous last words.

I was back up in the mess, sitting across from Nasha while she sipped a paste smoothie and went over in glorious detail all the things she was going to do to me once she was allowed to touch me again when she stopped midsentence to look over my shoulder. I turned. It was Burke. He was holding a tablet.

"Have you two exchanged fluids yet?"

"Not yet," Nasha said. "We're definitely going to, though."

"No," Burke said. "You're not."

He turned the tablet around so that we could both see it. There was an image there, a picture of a walnut cut in half, gray matter wrapped around white matter wrapped around . . .

"What is that?" I asked, though I was pretty sure I already knew the answer.

"It's your brain," Burke said.

"No shit," Nasha said. She leaned across the table and poked the dark curl in the center of the image with one finger. "What the fuck is *that*, asshole?"

"It's a tumor," I said. "I've got a brain tumor, right?"

"No," Burke said. "You definitely don't have a brain tumor. Your body is barely a week old. Brain tumors don't grow that fast."

"Fine," I said. "So what is it?"

"I don't know," Burke said, "but you're going back in the chamber until we find out."

So you remember I said that you don't want to die of a pulmonary hemorrhage? Well, here's another thing to add to your list of deaths to avoid: having your brain eaten from the inside out by parasitic worms.

It took the better part of a month for them to finish me off, but for the last week or so of that I was basically an empty shell. Weeks two and three, though, were not fun. It started with headaches, then seizures, then progressive dementia. By the end, the walls were talking to me, telling me that Nasha didn't really love me, that all my other iterations were in hell waiting for me, that the parasites were going to just keep eating and eating and never let me die.

That was a lie, anyway. They did let me die.

When it was over, the larvae came pouring out of my mouth and nose and ears, ready to move on to whatever the next stage of their life cycle was. We never found out what that might be, because Arkady sterilized the living shit out of them and then tossed the whole mess into the hopper to make a new me.

So yeah, after all that, you wouldn't think whatever Marshall has planned for me now would scare me, would you?

You wouldn't think so—but for some goddamned reason, it does.

THEY MARCH US down the spoke corridor toward the hub in a single-file line, with the smaller goon leading, the bigger one trailing, and Nasha, Eight, and me strung out in between. When we start down the central stairs my stomach knots as I suddenly wonder if we're actually going straight to the cycler. Apparently Nasha has the same thought, because when we pass the second level she says, "You know you can't take any disciplinary action against us until you have a judicial finding, right?"

"Oh please," the bigger goon says from behind us. "After what we just saw, you're lucky we didn't burn you down on the spot."

"Fuck you," Eight says. "What are you, a Natalist?"

"Yeah," he says, "and so is Marshall. You guys are screwed."

"He's not wrong," the one in front says without turning around.

"This colony wasn't chartered as a theocracy," Nasha says. "You can't just burn us at the stake."

The goon shrugs. "Guess that's up to Marshall."

When we get down to the ground level, they don't take us to the cycler. They don't take us to the dungeon either, because we don't have one. We don't even have a jail, as far as I know.

Instead, they take us to the Security ready room. It's an odd choice, because there are lockers there filled with body armor and weapons. There's also a miniature auto-caf. We could start an armed insurrection, and also have a nice snack. This seems like really poor planning on Security's part.

"Wait here," the bigger one says before closing us in. "Keep your hands off the equipment, and don't even think about ordering food."

"Or what?" Nasha says.

He stares at her for a long moment, then shakes his head and says, "Just wait here."

After he's gone, Nasha walks over to one of the lockers and shows her ocular to the scanner. The light on the display flashes red.

"Oh well," she says. "Worth a try."

"Nice," Eight says. "What would you have done if it'd opened?"

She shrugs. "Shot my way to freedom, I guess."

If we could get into the lockers, what would we do? It's an interesting question, actually. We're not even locked in here. Even without being able to get at weapons, we could run. We could try to jump one of the goons when they come back for us. We could do lots of things. What would it get us, though? This dome is the only place on this planet that won't kill us in short order. When I actually think about it, I start to realize that in some sense Niflheim itself is just a really big, really cold jail.

There's a couch in the center of the room, and a low coffee table. Eight drops down on one end, leans his head back, and closes his eyes. After a minute, I take the other. Nasha sits between us, pulls us toward her, and slings her arms around both of our shoulders.

"You know," she says, "if you'd asked me before we left Midgard how I thought I was going to die, shoved down the corpse hole for sex crimes wouldn't have been at the top of my list."

"You're not going down today," Eight says without opening his eyes. "We've only got two atmospheric pilots, and you're one of them. Marshall will find some way to make you miserable over this, but he can't kill you."

"I don't know," Nasha says. "He may think that way now, but what about after I murder Chen?"

Eight shrugs. "Depends on how hard you try to make it look like an accident, I guess."

We're quiet for a while then, the three of us, eyes closed and heads touching. Eight's probably right that Marshall won't kill Nasha. He definitely will kill the hell out of us, though, and at this point I'm pretty confident that when Nine comes out of the tank afterward, it won't be me looking out through his eyes, Ship of Theseus be damned.

Oh well. At least I'm in good company.

It's maybe an hour later when the smaller of the two goons who brought us here comes back.

"Barnes," he says, "let's go." He grimaces. "Both of you. Adjaya—you stay here for now."

Nasha still has her arms around us. She kisses Eight, then turns to kiss me. The goon turns away.

"What the hell, Adjaya? Seriously. What the hell?"

"Suck it," she says.

Eight sighs. "You know," he says, "you're not helping things here."

He's probably right. On the other hand, from our perspective at least, there's almost certainly no way to make things worse. We get to our feet, and we go.

HE DOESN'T TAKE us to the cycler. He takes us four doors down the corridor, and sticks us in another room about the size of a storage closet.

"What's this?" I ask.

He shrugs. "A storage closet."

He shoves us inside, then closes the door behind us. The room is dark. My ocular flips over to infrared, but I'd just as soon get some sleep at this point, so I flip it back. I hunch down in one corner and rest my forehead on my knees. I'm just drifting off when a chat window opens.

<Mickey8>: Ab**st nder**nd?

I flip my ocular back to IR and look up at Eight. He's in the opposite corner, hunched over just like me. He's already snoring.

<Mickey8>: Un***st**d

Ugh. He's sleep-texting. I blink the chat widow closed, shut my ocular down, and close my eyes.

I HAVE NO idea how long it's been when I wake to a flood of light from the open door. A new goon has come for us. This one I recognize. His name is Lucas. I used to see him in the carousel during transit, practicing some sort of martial art in extreme slow motion. I once asked him what the point of that was. I mean, isn't the whole key to winning a fight being faster than the other guy? He smiled and shook his head, and proceeded on to the next form.

He's always struck me as a decent sort, but he doesn't look happy to be dealing with us this morning.

"Hey," he says. "You're in some trouble here, Mickey."

"Yeah," Eight says. "We gathered."

"What happened to you, homes? How the hell did you wind up a multiple?"

"Long story," I say. "The short answer, though, is that this is all Berto's fault."

He laughs. "Should have known. Gomez is a piece of work. I never understood why you spent so much time with him."

"Yeah," Eight says. "I've been wondering that myself lately."

"Oh well," Lucas says. "Best get to your feet now. The big man wants to see you."

"GOOD LORD, BARNES," Marshall says. "Despite everything, I didn't want to believe it."

I decide not to ask what he means by "despite everything."

We're back in his office again, sitting in the same little chairs Berto and I were in a couple of days ago. The past forty-eight hours don't seem to have improved Marshall's mood.

"Look," Eight says. "I know this seems bad, sir, but it doesn't have to be the end of the world. I get that there shouldn't be two of us right now, but you know we didn't do it deliberately. And anyway, in some ways this is a good thing. The colony is barely at viability as it is, and the two of us can be twice as useful. At the end of the day, you need us. You need to let this slide."

Marshall's face reddens, and his jaw works silently for a long two seconds before he surges to his feet and slams his fists down onto his desk.

"Listen to me, you goddamned abomination! I don't give a *shit* about deliberately! Set aside the fact that you've stolen seventy kilos of vital calcium and proteins from a colony that's on the brink of starvation. Set aside the fact that one of you should have gone back into the cycler the goddamned *second* that you realized that you'd become a multiple. For the love of all that's holy, Barnes, you were having *relations* with one another. I don't . . . I . . ."

He sputters to a stop, then drops back into his chair. He takes a deep breath in, closes his eyes, and then lets it out slowly. When he opens them again, his expression is as blank as a mannequin's.

"You are a monster," Marshall says, his voice low and even, "and you are both going into the cycler. The only point of this discussion, the only questions we are trying to answer, are whether there will ever be a ninth iteration of you, and whether Adjaya should go down the corpse hole with you."

Eight's face goes slack at that, and I can feel my eyes widen.

"Sir," Eight says. "Please—"

"Nasha didn't know," I say. "I mean, she didn't know until I walked in on her with Eight, just before Security showed up to haul us away. You can't blame her, sir. This wasn't her fault."

"I've already spoken with Adjaya," Marshall says. "She claims that she did know, in fact. She claims that she realized something was off with you two days ago. She also let me know that what she was doing with the two of you is none of my goddamned business, and that I can shove my bullshit Natalist morality all the way up my ass sideways." He pauses for another deep, cleansing breath. "If she weren't one of our two qualified combat pilots, and if we were not currently facing the possibility of combat against hostile native sentients, she would have been gone already."

"Wait," Eight says. "What?"

"The prize you brought home from your snipe hunt two nights ago," Marshall says, "was not fully biological. The things you've been calling 'creepers' appear to actually be some sort of hybrid miltech. We suspected as much, of course, based on what they were able to do to the decking in the main lock, but our examination of the specimen has confirmed it. We are now on a war footing, which means that I'm going to have to think long and hard about what to do about Adjaya." He leans back in his chair, squeezes his eyes shut, and pinches the bridge of his nose. "Fortunately, I have no similar issues with the two of you." He gestures toward Lucas, who's been waiting just inside the door. "Take them to holding, please. I have a few more people I need to speak with. We'll sort them out when I'm done."

SO, FUN FACT: it turns out we do have a jail.

"WELL," EIGHT SAYS. "It's been a nice few days, anyway."

I get to my feet and walk the two steps from the bench to the bed. I had no idea until they tossed us in here that this colony even had a holding cell—apparently the goons who dragged us out of our room didn't either, or they wouldn't have risked their snack machine with us—but I guess it does. We're in a standard three-by-two room. The only difference between this place and all the other standard three-by-two rooms under the dome is that the door on this one locks from the outside.

As far as I can tell, we're the first two occupants it's had since we left Midgard.

"I guess our original plan was right, huh?" I drop onto the bed, lie back, and close my eyes. "You should have shoved me down the corpse hole when you had the chance. At least you would have done it headfirst."

"Yeah," he says. "I guess you're right about that. You think he's really gonna kill us both?"

"Seems like it."

We sit in silence for a while then. It's strange—in a way, this all almost comes as a relief. Ever since I walked into our room to find Eight in my bed covered in tank goo, I've had this knot of visceral dread hanging around in my stomach. I knew we wouldn't be able to keep this a secret forever, and I was terrified of what would happen when it came out. Now that it has, and I know more or less what's going to happen and when, I actually feel a little calmer. In fact, I'm almost dozing when Eight speaks again.

"He said he might not pull Nine out of the tank. You don't think he'd do that, do you? I mean, the colony needs an Expendable."

I open my eyes, and turn my head to look at him. "Did it look like Marshall cares?"

He starts to reply, hesitates, then shakes his head. "No. I guess not."

I close my eyes again. "Here's a better question: Does it matter?"

"What the hell is that supposed to mean?"

I sigh, sit up, and turn to face him. "You're not me, Eight. Isn't that obvious?"

He stares at me for a long five seconds before saying, "What's your point?"

"My point is that all that stuff Jemma crammed into our head back on Himmel Station—all the bits about immortality, anyway—that was all bullshit. This is it. The past six weeks are the only life I get, and the last few days are the only life you get. We're fucking mayflies, and when Marshall shoves us down the corpse hole, that's it for us. I don't care if he pulls Nine out of the tank or not, because even if he does, *Nine won't be me.* He'll just be some other guy who sleeps in my bed and eats my rations and gets his hands all over my stuff."

Eight shakes his head. "No. I don't buy it. Remember that Ship of Theseus thing? Remember Kant? If he thinks he's me, and everyone around him thinks he's me, and there's no way to prove that he's not me, then *he's me.* This stuff you're doing right now? This is exactly why they don't allow multiples."

I roll my eyes. "They don't allow multiples because Alan Manikova tried to take over the universe."

"Whatever."

He slouches down on the bench then, folds his arms across his chest, and closes his eyes.

Time passes. I doze and wake, doze and wake. Eight stays upright on the bench, eyes half-open mostly, hands folded in his lap. It occurs to me at one point that I'm sleeping away my last hours of existence, but I can't bring myself to care.

Eventually, the lock disengages with a *snick,* and the door swings open. A goon named Garrison steps inside. He's short and skinny and not carrying a burner, and for one stupid second I think about jumping him, overpowering him, busting out, and running.

Running where, though? Idiot.

"Hey," he says. "Which one of you is Seven?"

I glance over at Eight. He shrugs. I groan, sit up, and raise one hand.

"Great," he says. "Let's go."

I stand. Eight gives me a half smile. "See you on the other side, brother."

"Yeah," I say. We both know that the other side for us is somebody's mug of slurry, but at least it seems like he's forgiven me for pricking his immortality bubble. Garrison steps back and gestures down the corridor. I follow him out.

The cycler is on the bottom level, at the center of the dome. It quickly becomes obvious that's not where we're going. By the time we get to Marshall's office, I've started to wonder whether I might live another few hours after all.

It only occurs to me as Garrison is knocking on his door that maybe Marshall just wants to shoot me himself.

"Come," Marshall says. The door swings open, and Garrison waves me in. I step past him. The door closes behind me.

"Sit," Marshall says.

I shake my head. "I think I'd rather stand."

He sighs, lets his bloodshot eyes sag closed in a long blink, then opens them again. "Suit yourself, Barnes."

He leans back in his chair, drops his hands into his lap, and looks up at me. "I've been talking to Gomez. I need you to tell me what you know about those things out there."

"Things, sir? You mean the creepers?"

"Yes. In his initial report regarding your presumed loss, Gomez said that you'd been killed by them. In his amended report subsequent to our interview three days ago, he said that you were killed in a fall. An hour ago, he amended that explanation further to state that you did in fact fall through the ice into some sort of tunnel or cave system, but that you were still alive and conscious when he left you there. He estimated that you may have been as much as a hundred meters below the surface. He thought you'd died there, but clearly you managed to find your way back out, didn't you?"

I nod. "That's what caused this mess, sir. Berto reported me lost, and by the time I made it back to the dome, Eight was already out of the tank."

He cuts me off with a wave of his hand. "I don't care about that right now, Barnes. I care about these tunnels. They shouldn't be there. Our orbital surveys indicated that this entire area was completely geologically stable. No volcanism, no fault lines, no mountains, no soft rock. There's nothing here that would explain an extensive cave system."

"Yes, sir," I say. "I thought the same thing."

"Right. What was your impression when you were down there? Did it appear to be a natural geologic formation? Was there anything about what you saw that seemed artificial?"

I hesitate. How much to tell? How would Marshall react to knowing that there are creepers down there big enough to tear straight through the wall of the dome if they wanted to?

I don't have to wonder about that, actually. I know how he'd react. He'd kill them all, if he could think of a way to do it.

Marshall controls the output of a starship engine.

He could definitely think of a way to do it.

I wonder if someone on Roanoke had similar thoughts at some point.

"The tunnels did not appear natural to me, sir. They appeared to be deliberately structured."

His eyebrows come together over the bridge of his nose. "I see. And when, exactly, were you planning on mentioning this to someone?"

I don't respond. He obviously knows the answer. After an awkward five seconds, he waves the question off.

"Fine. I suppose I understand your hesitance to come forward, given your circumstances. Did you see anything alive down there?"

And this is the moment of truth, isn't it? I think about the giant creeper pushing me up that tunnel, setting me free in the garden. I think about the visions I've been having, about the caterpillar's Cheshire grin.

I think about Dugan, being pulled under the snow.

I think about Roanoke.

I close my eyes and breathe in, breathe out.

I tell him everything.

Eight's head snaps up when the door swings open. His jaw sags when he sees it's me.

"Hey," I say. "Did you miss me?"

Garrison locks us in again. I sit down on the bed.

Eight tilts his head to one side. "Explain?"

I shrug. "For the moment, it seems like Marshall is more worried about having his colony eaten by creepers than he is about having a perverted multiple hanging around."

"Huh," he says. "That's surprisingly sensible."

"To be clear, I didn't say he's not going to kill us. He's still pondering, I think. I told him what happened to me after Berto abandoned me. I think it spooked him."

"What *did* happen to you? You never told me."

"Let's just say that I wasn't surprised when Marshall told us that we're dealing with sentients. Also, just FYI, the kind we've seen aren't all there is. There are creepers out there that are big enough to eat a flitter and have room left over for dessert."

"And they've got miltech."

"Apparently."

"And we're moving to a war footing."

"That's what Marshall says."

He leans forward, rests his elbows on his knees, and rubs his face with both hands.

"This isn't good, Seven. We're not equipped for a ground war with a technological species. There's only a hundred and eighty of us."

"One-seventy-six. We're down five of everyone else, and up one of us."

He looks up at me and scowls. "Whatever. We needed to know this before we dropped the colony."

So that we could have bombarded the creepers from orbit, he means. So that we could have committed genocide before putting any of ourselves in harm's way.

I have to remind myself at this point that Eight is me, six weeks or so removed. How can I be so horrified at what he's saying? Have the creepers really gotten that far into my head?

"Doesn't matter," I say. "We didn't know, and it's too late to do anything about it now."

He leans back and folds his arms across his chest. "Is it?"

And that's it, of course. It might not be. As I said before— Marshall has the full energy output of a starship engine at his disposal. We may not have the high ground anymore, but we still have an insane amount of power available.

"Anyway," I say, "whatever winds up happening, I don't think either of us is going to be around to worry about it."

"I don't know," Eight says. "He hasn't killed us yet, right?"

I lie back on the bed again, fold my hands behind my head, and close my eyes.

"Don't get too excited, Eight. I'm pretty sure this is a temporary reprieve."

FOR SOME REASON, while I'm lying there in the holding cell waiting for Marshall to make up his mind about what to do with me and hoping that if he does decide to cycle me he at least has the decency to kill me first, I find myself thinking about Six.

I don't remember all of my deaths, obviously. Four refused to upload before he died, and I don't remember being Two at all. I know exactly what happened to both of them, though. I saw surveillance video of each of their endings. I'm still not sure which is worse, honestly—remembering your own death, or watching it on video. Six, though . . . I thought I knew what happened to him. Berto told me he got torn apart by creepers.

Berto told me *I* got torn apart by creepers.

Berto has demonstrated pretty clearly that he can't be trusted when it comes to me and dying.

I wonder now—did Six wind up abandoned in the tunnels too? Did he just never manage to find his way back out? If I ever get the chance to see Berto again, I'm gonna squeeze the truth out of him.

Even if it kills me.

I'm still contemplating that when my ocular pops open a chat window.

<Mickey8>: In**stan* cl**r?

I turn my head to look at Eight.

"Come on," he says. "Again with this shit?"

<Mickey8>:C*e*r? S**nder?

I sit up. "What are you doing, Eight?"

"Me? What are *you* doing? What's with the gibberish?"

I shake my head. "That's not me. I thought you were sleep-chatting."

His face shifts from annoyed to confused. "Sleep-chatting? Is that a thing?"

"Maybe?"

<Mickey8>: Un*r**nd? C***r?

I blink the window closed. "If that's not you, and it's not me, then who is it?"

Eight shrugs. "It's a glitch, obviously. There's not supposed to be two separate nodes in the system with identical handles. There must be some kind of feedback thing going on between us."

"Oh please," I say. "You're making that up. You don't know any more than I do about the network, and I don't have any idea whether what you're saying is even plausible."

"Tell you what," he says. "After Marshall shoves you down the corpse hole, I'll see if he'll hold off on me for a while so I can check to see if it's still happening. Should be an interesting experiment."

I sigh. "Thanks, Eight. You're a pal."

YOU MIGHT HAVE the impression at this point that every colony that's ever been attempted has failed miserably. That's not remotely true, obviously. I've been perseverating on the failures because that's where my head has been pretty much ever since we entered orbit around Niflheim, but there have been tons of rousing successes. Take Bergen's World, for example.

Bergen's World was jungle from pole to pole when the first colony ship arrived. It had two continents, one huge and one smaller, both straddling the equator on opposite sides of the planet, with warm blue oceans, a whole mess of jungle islands, an atmosphere rich in oxygen and thick with CO_2, and a biosphere that could best be described as maniacal. There weren't any sentients and there wasn't anything alarmingly large, but the animals were fast and strong and bad-tempered, the trees were semi-motile and carnivorous, and the microbiota was adaptive, infectious, and omnipresent. Command dropped a small exploratory party from orbit, just to get the lay of the land.

Even with armor and heavy weapons, they didn't last a day.

The inhospitality of the place put the Bergen's World Command in a bit of a pickle. As I've mentioned, colony ships don't really have the option of packing up and heading to a new destination once they've settled down. So they made the best of it.

They sterilized the smaller continent. Burned it down damn near to the bedrock.

It's a beautiful place now. Practically a paradise, from everything I've read.

So, yeah, it's not true that every time we make landfall on a new planet we wind up dying.

I mean, *somebody* almost always does.

It's just not necessarily us.

IT'S CLOSING IN on noon when the door opens again. It's a different goon this time—a bigger guy, with dark skin and a clean-shaven head. His name is Tonio. I'm pretty sure he was the one who tased me in the cafeteria two days ago.

"On your feet," he says. "Let's go."

"Which one of us?" Eight asks.

"Both."

I look over at Eight. He shrugs. We get to our feet, and we go.

It's funny how expectations work. Four hours ago, I left the cell expecting to go to the cycler. I wasn't afraid, really. I knew what was going to happen, and I knew there was nothing I could do about it. There's a certain peace that comes with that.

This time, I leave the cell assuming that we're headed back to Marshall's office to talk about creepers. We're not, though. We pass that corridor and keep walking. My heart lurches, and my stomach twists itself into an aching knot.

This time, we really are going to the cycler.

Marshall is there waiting for us when we arrive, along with Nasha and Cat and two other goons. These ones are carrying burners.

The corpse hole is open. Tiny flashes of light dance across its surface.

"So," Marshall says. "Before we get started, I have a few questions."

"Oh, for shit's sake," Eight mutters.

Marshall's eyes narrow. "Excuse me?"

"Look," Eight says. "I know you, Marshall. I've been getting myself killed for you for nine years now. Despite that, for the most part you're a decent guy. You've got a stick up your ass most of the time, but you're not some kind of villain from a vid drama, and I don't know why you're trying to act like one now. You don't want a multiple hanging around your colony. Fine. Kill one of us, and shove him down the hole. Problem solved. Or kill both of us and pop a new one out of the tank, if that's the way you want to go. Just do it, and quit dicking around."

"Well," Marshall says. "Just to be clear—if the two of you wind up going down the hole today, there will never be another of you. Your personality will be wiped from the server, as will your body template. You're not looking at a trip to the tank right now, Barnes. You're looking at a death sentence."

Eight shakes his head. "Bullshit. There are only a hundred and seventy-six of us left, and we're moving to a war footing. You need every body you can get right now. You sure as shit can't throw away your only Expendable."

"This is true," Marshall says, and his face breaks into a tight-lipped smile. "What is not true is that you are the only person in this colony who is willing and able to fill the role of Expendable. In fact, Corporal Chen has graciously volunteered to take your berth, if and when that becomes necessary."

Eight opens his mouth, closes it, then opens it again, all without speaking. I turn to look at Cat and her Security pals. The other two are eyeing me, fingers tickling the triggers of their burners, but Cat's staring down at the floor in front of her.

"Cat?"

"I'm sorry," she says without looking up. "It's nothing personal, Mickey. It's for the good of the colony."

I bark out a short, sharp laugh. "The good of the colony. Right. This is what you were on about the other night, isn't it? Do I think I'm immortal? I guess you've got your answer to that now, huh?"

She meets my eyes. The anguish in her face drains the anger out of me.

"Please, Mickey. I didn't mean for all of this to happen."

"You *made* all of this happen, Cat."

A tear leaks from the corner of her eye and trails down her cheek. "I'm sorry," she says. "I just . . ."

"Shut up," Nasha says. "Seriously, Chen. Just shut the fuck up."

"Enough!" Marshall says. "There's no point in acting as if this is some kind of betrayal, Barnes. As I understand it, Chen became aware of your situation through your actions, not hers. Once that happened, she was bound by duty to report to Command. If she hadn't done so, she'd be standing beside you right now, waiting to go down the hole. Moreover, her decision to volunteer to replace you has no bearing whatsoever on what eventually becomes of you. If I decide to wipe you, we'll either find a volunteer to replace you, or we'll draft one." He pauses to wait for that to sink in before continuing. "The salient point right now, however, is that you still have an opportunity to make sure that doesn't happen."

The room falls silent. Behind us, one of the goons resets the safety on his burner with an audible click.

Eight is the first one to speak. "What do we have to do?"

"Nothing out of the ordinary," Marshall says. "All you need to do to avoid going down that hole is to fulfill your duty. I have a mission for you."

I roll my eyes. "A mission which will result in both of us being killed, I assume?"

Marshall turns to me, and his smile turns into a smirk. "Do I need to refer you back to your job description, Mr. Barnes?"

I sigh. "Tell me."

And so, he does.

ANTIMATTER, IN CASE you were wondering, is a hell of a thing.

When it's kept to itself, it basically behaves like regular matter. If there had been a hair more antimatter created during the Big Bang and a hair less normal matter, we could have a perfectly functional antimatter universe right now. There wasn't, though. Because of that, we have a normal matter universe, and when antimatter is brought into it, bad things happen. It's not quite true that you get a pure conversion of mass to energy when normal matter and antimatter interact, but depending on exactly what kind of particles are interacting, what their energy states were before they met one another, and what sort of environment they're in, you can get anything from a barrage of gamma rays to a massive spew of subatomic particles ricocheting around at a significant fraction of the speed of light.

As either One or Two would have been happy to tell you, as a living organism, you really don't want to be anywhere near any of those things.

Antimatter was discovered back on old Earth, pre-Diaspora, well before the *Ching Shih* was even a gleam in someone's autoCAD. For a long time, though, it was mostly just a curiosity. They didn't figure out how to synthesize and contain it in any significant quantity until just before the breakout. In fact, most people would argue that the Chugunkin Process was the singular advancement that led most directly to the Diaspora.

Partially that's because antimatter is absolutely critical for interstellar travel. Nothing else that our physics has yet discovered contains enough energy in a compact-enough form to get us anywhere near the speeds that we need to cross the gulfs between stars. Still, even if that weren't true—if, for example, some of the reactionless thrust concepts they were playing with before Chugunkin did his thing had actually paid out—it seems pretty likely that the Diaspora wouldn't have happened without the ability to create antimatter in bulk.

It should be pretty clear by now that launching a colony mission is in most ways a desperate act. It's expensive, it has a high probability of failure, and even if it succeeds, the place you're going to will probably be significantly worse than the place you came from for at least a few lifetimes. In order to make a leap like that, you have to either be running *toward* something great, or running *away* from something truly terrifying. For the ancient Micronesians, the thing they were running from was resource depletion and starvation.

The thing that we're running from is the Bubble War.

It's a truism that every new technological advancement in human history has been applied first to advance the interests of the horny. The printing press? Some Bibles, mostly porn. Antibiotics? Perfect for treating STIs. The ocular? Don't get me started on what those were first used for. Large-scale antimatter production didn't really fit that model, though. There's nothing remotely sexy about a rapidly expanding cloud of high-speed quarks and gluons.

The second area where every new technology is applied, of course, is war.

In that space, antimatter worked out heinously well.

In fairness, our ancestors did spend about ten seconds or so thinking about how antimatter could be used for things like energy production and starship propulsion before they turned their attention to the ways it could be used to convert their fellow humans into radioactive dust. I'm guessing, though, that the main reason for that was that until the invention of the magnetic monopole bubble, there wasn't any practical way to use antimatter as a tool of genocide. You can't just make an antimatter bomb the way you can a thermonuclear bomb, for example. You need a way to keep your antimatter core completely isolated from any interaction with normal matter until you want it to do its thing, and absent a five-thousand-kilo magnetic torus and a vacuum chamber to keep it in, that's pretty difficult to do.

The magnetic monopole bubble solved that problem neatly. As Jemma explained it to me, each one is a kind of knot in space-time, with the interior and exterior essentially existing in separate universes. Wrap a little dollop of antimatter up in one of those, and you've got a whole lot of potential energy stored in a compact and relatively safe-to-handle package. That's how the *Drakkar* stored her fuel. When she was under acceleration, a steady stream of monopole bubbles filled with antimatter were passed through from containment into the reaction chamber, where they were mixed with opposite-polarity bubbles filled with normal matter.

Then, two by two, the bubbles popped. Annihilation occurred, and off we went.

You can probably see where this is going.

The bubble bomb is a very simple thing. You just pack a bunch of monopole bubbles full of antimatter into some kind of delivery device. When that device bursts over the target, the bubbles drift with the wind, forced apart from one another by their mutual magnetic repulsion. After a fixed amount of time, they pop.

Depending on how much dispersion you've allowed and what specific type of antimatter you've packed into your bubble, the result can range from an explosion that blows a hole through the stratosphere, to a rain of hard radiation and quantum particles that kills every living thing in the target area down to the viral level, but leaves the buildings and other infrastructure completely intact.

It was that bit that caught the attention of old Earth war planners. They'd had thermonuclear weapons for a long while by then, but they hadn't figured out a way to make them useful for anything other than an apocalyptic suicide pact. The problem was that if you ever used enough of them to deliver a knockout blow, the environmental blowback in terms of fallout, garbage thrown into the stratosphere, lingering background radiation, etc., etc., meant that you'd wind up killing not just your target, but also their neighbors, their neighbors' neighbors, their neighbors' neighbors' neighbors, and so on back to probably yourself—and that's assuming that your victims didn't have their own doomsday arsenal to throw back at you, which they probably did if you were contemplating that kind of escalation against them in the first place.

The bubble bomb solved all of those problems. Structured and deployed correctly, it allowed you to sterilize wide swaths of your enemy's landmass with almost no lingering side effects. You could make the bombs small and light and deliver them stealthily enough that the enemy wouldn't know they were coming until they were already dead. You could kill everyone and everything, and then move right in and take over the next day if you wanted to. You didn't even need to worry about the bodies stinking, because there wouldn't be any viable bacteria around to make them decay. From a warfighter's perspective, it was the perfect weapon.

From an actual human being's perspective, of course, it was a nightmare.

The critical context here is that old Earth was undergoing a bit of an environmental crisis at the time that all this was going on. Their population density was almost a hundred times greater than Eden's is now, which is more like a thousand times the average density of most of the Diaspora, and their industry and agriculture were a lot more inefficient and messy than ours are. As a result, they were basically choking on their own waste. Over the course of a few hundred years they'd altered their atmospheric chemistry to the point that whole chunks of the planet that were once heavily populated were rapidly becoming uninhabitable, and they were having serious issues with distribution of both food and water. Combine this with the fact that they were also completely fractured politically—there were nearly two hundred independent political entities claiming sovereign rights over one part of the planet or another—and then throw in the sudden appearance of a weapon that allowed one of those entities to eliminate the population of another completely, and subsequently to move into their newly empty territory, and you've obviously got the makings of a very bad situation.

Records of the Bubble War are probably not particularly reliable, since they were almost entirely written by the folks who struck first and hardest and therefore survived, but there are a few things that we know for certain. The war lasted, in total, less than three weeks. Only a half dozen or so of those independent political entities participated. It ended only when the planet's existent supply of antimatter was exhausted.

Most importantly, it left more than half of old Earth's population, which at the time was all there was of us, dead or dying.

Most historians think that the launch of the *Ching Shih,* which took place less than twenty years later, was a direct reaction to the Bubble War. What else could explain the Diaspora? What else could explain the fact that we left the one planet in all of creation that we were actually evolved to inhabit, the one that didn't require any terraforming or inoculations or wars with native sentients, for . . . well, for places like Niflheim? It was clear to those people that if humanity stayed in one place, we'd eventually kill one another—and they were almost certainly right. Nobody has heard a peep out of old Earth in over six hundred years.

Our only hope for long-term survival was to spread.

It was also clear to them that the Diaspora would be futile if antimatter weapons came with it. We've ostracized old Earth from the start of the Union, and at this point we don't even know if there's anyone left alive there. We like to think that we're different from them, that we're more enlightened or evolved or some such bullshit.

It's not true, though. The people of the Union are no different, at the end of the day, from the ones of old Earth. We still argue with one another. We still sometimes fight.

We don't do it with antimatter, though. That's the one hard and fast rule, even deeper-seated in our psyches than the ban on multiples, that every world in the Union abides by.

That's the one rule that, if it's broken and one of the neighboring worlds finds out about it, will buy you a *Bullet.*

"THIS IS THE place, right?" Berto asks from the cockpit.

The bay door slides open, and I look down. We're hovering over a crevasse. It looks pretty much like every other crevasse in this godforsaken place. Is this where I fell?

"Maybe," I say. "Who knows?"

"I'll take that as a yes," Berto says.

The drop winch deploys two meters of cable. Eight shoulders his pack and clips in.

"See you down there," he says, and steps into space.

I lift my own pack as the cable plays out. It's not as heavy as I expected.

Hard to believe it carries enough destructive force to sterilize a city.

Soon enough, the winch reverses. When the end of the cable appears, though, I hesitate.

"Hey," I say. "Berto? Before I do this, there's one thing that I'd really appreciate you clearing up. What actually happened to Six?"

Berto sighs. "Creepers took him, Mickey. I told you that the first time you asked, right after you came out of the tank."

"I don't believe that," I say. "You told me that creepers ate me, remember?"

"I didn't say they *ate* him," Berto says. "I said they *took* him. You inferred the eating thing. He was working another crevasse, not too far from here. They came up out of the snow, just like I said. They didn't rip him up, though. They dragged him down a hole. It was fifteen minutes before I lost his signal. He was incoherent for the last ten. I got the impression . . ."

"What?" I say.

"I'm pretty sure they were doing what we did to that creeper you hauled in," Berto says. "They were taking him apart to see how he worked."

"They took his ocular," I say. "They took *my* ocular."

"Maybe," Berto says. "Not like they could do anything with it."

Until the last few days, I would have agreed. Now, though?

"You lied to me," I say. "You lied to *Command*. You must have known the creepers were sentient before I did. You could have gotten cycled for that, Berto. What were you thinking?"

He doesn't answer. I wait through a long ten seconds, then shake my head and reach for the cable.

"I was afraid," Berto says.

I turn to look at him. He won't meet my eyes.

"Afraid of what? Until you falsified your reports, you hadn't done anything wrong. What happened to me wasn't your fault."

"No," he says. "I wasn't afraid of Command. I was afraid of those fucking creepers. I could have saved you, probably. I could have pulled you back out of that hole. I could maybe even have saved Six if I'd gotten to ground quick enough, and brought along an accelerator. I didn't, though. I didn't, because I was afraid."

And now, suddenly, it all makes sense.

"You're Berto Gomez," I say. "You're the guy who flies a flitter through a three-meter gap at two hundred meters per second. You're not afraid of anything."

He sighs, and nods.

"You risked actually getting cycled because you couldn't admit to me, to Marshall . . . to yourself? You couldn't let anyone know that there was something out there that frightened you."

He turns back to the controls. "Eight is waiting for you, Mickey."

"You know," I say, "if any of me makes it through into Nine somehow, I'm gonna make a point first thing of kicking the crap out of you."

He doesn't have anything to say to that.

I clip in, and I go.

"So," Eight says when I unclip at the bottom. "*Is* this the place?"

I look around. The floor of the crevasse is maybe a half dozen meters wide. Thirty meters of ice loom over us on both sides. Halfway up one wall, a boulder that looks a little like a monkey's head juts out of the ice.

"Yeah," I say. "I think so. Don't think it really matters, though. I'm pretty sure this whole area is undermined. If this isn't exactly where I went down before, we just need to find another entrance to the tunnels."

The cable disappears, and a few moments later we hear the hum of gravitics as Berto's shuttle accelerates away. We start walking. Just past the boulder, I see the edge of the hole. Apparently it hasn't snowed enough in the past few days to cover it over.

"There," I say. "That's where I fell."

We walk up to the edge and look down into a steep, slanting, rock-walled tunnel a bit more than a meter wide.

"Looks climbable," Eight says.

"Eight," I say. "We shouldn't do this."

He turns to look at me. "You think there's a better way in?"

"No," I say. "That's not what I mean. I mean that we shouldn't do this."

"Yes," he says. "We should."

"The creepers," I say. "They're sentients." I hook one thumb toward my pack. "And these things are war crimes. If Midgard finds out that we did this, they'll make us the next Gault."

Each of our packs, for all intents and purposes, contains a miniature bubble bomb: fifty thousand tiny nuggets of antimatter taken from what's left of the *Drakkar*'s fuel stores, each one isolated in a magnetic monopole bubble. When we release them, they'll disperse, drifting through the air like will-o'-the-wisps.

Eventually, the bubbles will pop.

The fact of what I'm carrying on my back right now is making my skin crawl.

"I know they're sentients," Eight says. "That's why we have to do this—and it's only a war crime if we use these weapons on humans. Anything goes on a beachhead. Our terraformers have sterilized entire continents to make space for us where they had to. You know this." He sits down at the edge of the hole and leans forward. "Give me a hand, huh? It's a bit of a drop to the first ledge."

"One of them saved me," I say.

He looks up at me. "What?"

"Four days ago," I say. "When I got lost in these tunnels, and Berto gave me up for dead. One of the creepers saved me. It picked me up and carried me almost back to the dome. It let me go."

"So what you're saying," Eight says, "is that all of this bullshit that's happened to us is actually *their* fault."

Okay. I guess that's one way of looking at it.

"Anyway," Eight says, "it doesn't matter. You heard what Marshall said. If we don't do this, we go into the cycler, and we don't get to come back out. He wipes our personality off the server, and fucking *Chen* takes our place." He inches a bit farther forward, and looks down again. "You know what? I think I've got this." He braces one hand on either side of the opening, lifts himself up, and lets his legs dangle. "Meet me at the bottom, huh?"

He lowers himself down into the hole and disappears.

I stand there, staring down into the hole, for a long while. I could just walk away, I think—wander off into the snow, pop the seals on my rebreather, and be done with it.

Wouldn't make a difference, though, would it? They'd send Berto or Nasha out to find my body, retrieve the pack, and send Nine down into the tunnels with it, assuming that Eight hadn't already finished the job.

Eventually, my ocular pings.

<Mickey8>:Let's go, Seven. We've got things to do.

I sigh, tighten the straps on my pack, and follow him down.

"WE SHOULD SPLIT up," Eight says. "Get as far away from one another as we can, then pull our triggers simultaneously. That way we get maximum spread, and we shouldn't have to worry about the blast from one of our weapons screwing with the dispersal pattern of the other."

"Eight—" I begin, but he shakes his head.

"No," he says. "I don't want to hear it. Start walking. Keep a voice channel open. When you're ready to do it, let me know. And if you run into your friend from the other day . . ." He turns away. "I don't know. Tell him we're sorry."

I stand there watching his heat signature fade long after he's disappeared down one of the side tunnels. Maybe I think he'll

come back? He doesn't, though. Eventually, I pick a tunnel of
my own, snug the straps of my pack down to my shoulders, and
start walking.

"SEVEN. YOU THERE?"

"Yeah. I'm here."

"You seeing anything? These tunnels seem pretty empty."

"Nope. I've been hearing things off and on, though."

"Yeah, me too. Scratching behind the walls, right?"

"Right. That's our friends, I'd guess."

"Think they know we're here?"

I roll my eyes, though I know he can't see it. "This is their
house, Eight. How long would it take us to figure out that one of
them had gotten into the dome?"

The silence stretches on, until I begin to wonder whether he's
cut the connection.

"Think they know what we're here to do?"

IT'S TEN MINUTES later, and I'm standing at a crossroads trying
to decide whether I should take the upward-slanting route or the
one that spirals down when my comm flashes. A still frame pops
up in the upper left corner of my FOV. It's a broad, deep cavern
seen from high above.

Every square meter of it is covered in creepers.

They're the smaller ones, the kind that took down Dugan and
ripped through the floor of the main lock.

There must be thousands of them.

Tens of thousands.

"Seven! Seven, are you seeing this?"

"I see it," I say. "Eight, listen . . ."

I trail off then. Listen to what? I think back to that spider I set
loose in my mother's garden all those years ago. If it had come

back into the house, would I have saved it again, or would I have just crushed it and been done with it?

And what if I'd found a nest of spiders out there, hundreds of them, and realized they'd come to colonize the garden?

"Eight?"

Eight doesn't answer.

"Eight? You there?"

A final image drops into my cache. It's almost too blurred to interpret. I'd guess most people seeing this would have no idea what they were looking at.

I recognize it, though. It's the maw and feeding arms of a giant creeper, seen from no more than a couple of meters away.

That's when I realize that Eight is dead.

What now? I have no idea where he was, no idea how far away the crèche might be.

No idea if he had time to pull the trigger before they took him.

These tunnels are a blind maze. I could be kilometers from where Eight died, or it could be around the next bend.

I could try to find him.

I could pull the trigger now, and be done.

I close my eyes, start to reach for the cord, then hesitate.

There before me is the campfire, burning backward, sucking in smoke and turning ash into wood.

There before me is the caterpillar. The grin is gone, though. Its eyes are narrowed, and its mouth is a thin, hard line.

A chat window opens in the corner of my FOV.

<Mickey8>: Understa*d?

I open my eyes.

Something moves in the darkness.

Something that nearly fills the tunnel.

<Mickey8>: You understand?

I blink, run my tongue across my teeth, and swallow. My hand rests lightly on the trigger cord.

<Mickey8>: Yes, I understand.
<Mickey8>: You are Prime?

Okay, that I don't understand. The creeper moves closer. Both pairs of mandibles are spread wide. That has to be a threat posture, right? I take an involuntary step backward, and my hand tightens on the cord.

<Mickey8>: You are Prime?

I shake my head. Idiot. Even if it understood human body language, this thing probably doesn't have eyes.

<Mickey8>: We have destroyed your Ancillary. You are Prime?

Prime? Ancillary?
It's talking about Eight.
I could pull the trigger now.
I could, but I don't.
Instead, I take a leap of faith.

<Mickey8>: Yes, I am Prime.

The creeper's head settles to the tunnel floor, and the mandibles slowly close, inner first, then outer.

<Mickey8>:I am Prime also. We talk?

And so, we do.

IN ALL THE hundreds of worlds that make up the Union, there's only one where humans and native sentients have managed to coexist. It's a lonely little dwarf planet orbiting a gas giant, that is itself orbiting an M-class star at the far end of the spiral arm, almost twenty lights from the next-nearest colony. The mission that brought our people there was the single longest successful jump that we've managed. They named the planet Long Shot.

There's a whole other story behind that.

The natives on Long Shot are tree-dwelling cephalopods. I've seen vids of them zipping from branch to branch, changing colors on the fly to blend in with the canopy so effectively that you can really only see them in the infrared. Their population is concentrated in the central highlands of the planet's only continent. At the time of landfall they were scientifically and culturally advanced, but materially not much farther along than humans were prior to the development of agriculture. There's been a great deal of speculation over exactly why that is. The best explanation I've seen is that the entire reason humans wound up developing spears and houses and flitters and starships is that we were lousy at being regular animals.

The natives on Long Shot were not lousy at being regular animals. They had completely mastered their environment, and they hadn't needed rifles to do it. They ignored the colonists when they landed, because the beachhead was on the coast, hundreds of klicks from their mountains. The colonists ignored them because the natives were shy, localized, and nearly invisible, and for the first twenty years post-landfall, we had no idea they were there.

The histories don't say much about why this encounter turned out so differently from all the others. I've got a theory, though: by the time they finally bumped into one another, the colonists were well established enough to stop being constantly afraid.

Time. That's the key.

We just need time.

FOR THE SECOND time, for reasons that I still don't and probably never will understand, I walk alive out of the creepers' tunnels and into the low winter sun.

It's a beautiful morning by Niflheim standards. The sky is a clear light ocher with just a hint of blue, and the sun makes the snow between here and the dome look like a field of diamonds. I take a deep breath in, hitch up my pack, and start walking.

The snow is knee-deep, with drifts up to my waist, and even with the rebreather I'm not getting nearly as much oxygen out of Niflheim's atmosphere as my muscles are demanding, so I've got a good long while to game out how this is likely to go while I slog the kilometer or so back to the perimeter. I think about letting them know I'm coming. I even pop open a chat window before realizing that, no, that might tempt Marshall to try to stop me. If he ordered it, would Nasha or Berto be willing to drop a plasma bomb on my head?

Nasha wouldn't. I'm confident of that. Berto, though?

I honestly have no idea what would happen to the bundle of death on my back if he did.

Probably best for everyone if we don't find out.

I swing my route around so that I'm approaching, as near as I can make it, exactly between two pylons. I'd like to make it all the way to the dome before being challenged, but considering that the place is on high alert for creeper incursions I guess that's a lost hope. As it happens, I'm still a hundred meters out from the perimeter proper when both of the nearest pylons come to life. I keep walking as lights flash around their bases, and the burners rise from their peaks and swing around to orient on me.

"Don't," I say over the general comm channel, and hold up the trigger cord in my right hand. "Please. I don't want to pull this."

The burners don't withdraw, but they don't fire either. After what feels like hours but is probably actually more like thirty seconds, Marshall's voice speaks in my ear.

"Remove the pack, Barnes. Set it down carefully, and step away."

My hand on the cord starts shaking, and I have to stifle a giggle rising in the back of my throat.

"No," I say when I've got control of my voice. "I don't think I'll do that."

The comm cuts, this time for almost a minute. When the line opens again, I can hear the barely suppressed fury in Marshall's voice.

"Which one are you?"

"Seven," I say. "I'm Mickey7."

"Where is Eight?"

"Dead."

"Did he trigger his weapon?"

"No," I say. "He did not."

The comm cuts again. I glance over at the nearer of the two pylons. There's a dull red glow in the center of the barrel. I've never seen that before.

Which is to say, I guess, that I've never stared into the mouth of a primed burner before.

What would happen if it opened up on me? With a handheld burner I'm sure I'd have time to pull the cord before I died, even if it took me full in the face. With this thing, though?

Doesn't matter. Even if I died instantly, my arm might spasm. They can't risk it.

Can they?

I'm contemplating that question when a chat window opens.

<RedHawk>:Mickey? What the shit are you doing, man?

Oh well. At least he's not in a cockpit right now, getting ready to drop ordnance on me.

<Mickey8>:Hey there, Berto. Surprised to see me?

<RedHawk>:Seriously, Mickey. Have you gone completely insane? What are you trying to accomplish?

<Mickey8>:Send Marshall out here. We need to talk.

<RedHawk>:...

<Mickey8>:Not joking, Berto. Send him out.

<RedHawk>:Come on, Mickey. You know that's not gonna happen.

<Mickey8>:It is, Berto.

<RedHawk>:Take off the pack, Mick. That thing you're carrying ... it's a war crime. If you pull that cord, you'll be killing every human left on this planet. You don't want to do this.

<Mickey8>:Yeah. I'm pretty sure I led with "I don't want to do this." I don't want to kill you. Well, actually I kind of do want to kill you. I don't want to kill Nasha, though, or Cat, or even that asshole Tonio from Security. I don't want to kill anybody other than maybe you. What I want is to talk to Marshall, face-to-face. Send. Him. Out.

The window snaps closed, and I'm left to contemplate the burners on the pylons again.

They leave me standing there for almost an hour, staring up into that dull red glow while the cold seeps through the layers of my thermals, down into my skin and muscles, and finally straight through to my bones. Here is a hard, true fact: if you're left standing still for long enough in subzero weather, you will eventually be miserably, unbearably, bone-rattlingly cold, no matter how many layers of high-tech heat-retaining clothing you happen to be wearing. After forty minutes or so I find myself wishing that they'd just go ahead and open up on me with the burners so that at least I can die warm.

They don't, though. Instead, just when I've almost decided to pull the cord and be done with it, the secondary lock on the dome cycles open two hundred meters distant, and Marshall comes stomping out.

I think it's Marshall, anyway. It's a little difficult to tell through the rebreather and goggles and half dozen layers of cold-weather gear. The height is about right, though, and he's followed through the lock by two goons in full combat armor, so by the time that's all done with, I'm pretty confident it's him. I open a comm channel.

"Seriously? What's the escort for, Marshall? You've already got two cannons trained on me. How much more firepower do you think you need?"

"The security officers," he replies, his voice a low growl, "are here because I strongly suspect that this may be some sort of ambush."

I almost laugh at that. "An ambush? By who?"

"We are at war," Marshall says. "And for reasons that I honestly cannot fathom, you seem to have taken the enemy's side."

I don't have anything to say to that, so I stand silent and shivering, and watch him struggle toward me through the snow. He stops just at the perimeter, maybe ten meters away. The two goons stop a half pace behind him.

"Well?" Marshall says. "Here I am, Barnes. Do what you came here to do."

I wonder what he expects now. For me to wave my arms, I suppose, and summon an army of creepers up out of the snow to eat him. For just a moment I actually consider shouting, *Get him*, just to see what he'd do, but the goons both have accelerators at the ready, and they're probably nervous. This isn't the time for fun.

"I didn't do it," I say. "I didn't pull the trigger."

"I can see that," Marshall says. "What about your . . . friend?"

"You mean Eight?"

"Yes. Eight. Did he trigger his device?"

"No," I say. "I already told you that he didn't. He was killed before he could."

"I see," Marshall says. "What happened to his device?"

"The creepers have it."

The silence following that one stretches on for what feels like an eternity.

"Do they know what they have?" Marshall finally asks. There's a tremor in his voice that wasn't there before.

"Yes," I say. "They do."

"How do you know that?" Marshall asks.

"Because I told them what it was, and how it operates."

Marshall turns to the goon on his left. "Kill him."

"Sir?"

It's Cat. I should have recognized her armor. Marshall raises one trembling hand to point at me.

"This man has betrayed our colony, Corporal Chen. He has betrayed the Union. He has betrayed humanity. I have no doubt at this point that our time left on this planet will be measured in hours, if not minutes, but before that clock runs out I want to see him dead. Kill him."

"That's not a good idea," the goon on Marshall's other side says. It's Lucas, I think, but his voice is hard to make out over the comm. "He's carrying a bubble bomb, sir."

"Listen," I say. "I had to tell them what they had. Otherwise, they might have tried to take it apart, tried to see what makes it tick. If they'd done that—"

"If they'd done that," Marshall says, "this problem would have taken care of itself."

"Unless they decided to do it underneath the dome," Cat says. "That's what I would have done if I were them."

"It doesn't matter what you would have done," Marshall says. "It doesn't matter what justifications Barnes has dreamed up for what he's already done. This man has conspired with the enemy in a time of war. There is no greater crime."

"What about genocide?" I say. "That's a pretty great crime. It wasn't conspiring with the enemy that led us to abandon old Earth, you know. Also, not for nothing, we're not at war."

Marshall rounds back on me. "Those things out there have killed five of my people, you monster! Hell, they've killed *you* twice now. We've killed them as well. If we're not at war, then what are we?"

I shake my head. "You're thinking like a human. The creepers don't see it that way. They don't seem to have much of a concept of individual life. As far as I can tell, they're a communal intelligence. They don't care at all about the creepers we've killed, and they don't have an inkling of why we'd care about the people they've taken. The idea that dissecting a few ancillaries would be considered an act of aggression is beyond them. As far as they're

concerned, all we've done so far is exchange a bit of informa-
tion."

"Ancillaries?" Cat says.

"Yeah," I say. "That's my best translation for what they call
the little ones that we've seen around the dome. They're just parts
of the whole, not intelligent things themselves. They've been assuming that individual humans are the same."

"Great," Cat says. "Did you at least correct them on that?"

"I tried. Their grasp of the language is surprisingly good considering that everything they know, they've learned from snoop-
ing on my comms, but where the concepts aren't there, there's not
much you can do to translate. Anyway, they say they're sorry."

Cat starts to say something more, but Marshall cuts her off.

"Enough! Be silent, Chen, or by God you'll go down the corpse
hole with him."

"I'm not going down the corpse hole," I say.

"Oh, you are. Unless we're all blown to hell first, you are definitely going down the hole, and I do not care in the least if you're
alive or dead when it happens. You have to take that pack off
sometime, Barnes, and the minute you do, I'll put a round in you
myself."

"Not to criticize," Lucas says, "but you're not giving him a lot
of incentive not to kill us all right now, sir."

Marshall turns to glare at him, then Chen, then back at me.

"You can't kill me," I say. "Much though you might want to,
you can't. I'm your only liaison to the creepers, and they've got
an antimatter weapon now, just like we do."

"Thanks to you," he says. "Thanks to you, Barnes. You've
killed us all, you bastard."

I shake my head. "Sending a doomsday weapon down into
their tunnels wasn't my idea, and it wasn't my fault that they

took Eight before he could pull the trigger. That's on you, Marshall."

"But you could have ended it," he says. "If you'd just done your goddamned job, this would all be over. You're an Expendable, you coward, and you were afraid to die."

I sigh, and let my eyes fall closed. When I open them again, Cat and Lucas have shouldered their weapons.

"Maybe," I say. "Maybe I didn't want to die . . . or maybe I just didn't want to have a genocide on my conscience when I did. I get that you think I should have just pulled the cord, and killed the creepers, and died—but I didn't, and now we've got to move on from there. There's another intelligent species on this planet, and you've just handed them an antimatter weapon. You're in desperate need of diplomacy, and I'm your only diplomat. Do you really think killing me is in anybody's best interests at this point?"

Marshall stares me down for a solid thirty seconds. His hands are shaking and I can see his jaw working under his rebreather, but he doesn't say a word. In the end, he turns on his heel and stalks back toward the lock. Cat and Lucas stand and watch him go.

"So?" I say when the outer door cycles shut behind him. "Are we good?"

Cat glances over at Lucas. He turns to look at the nearest pylon. As we watch, the burner goes dark and sinks back onto its bearings.

"Yeah," Cat says. "I think so. For the moment, anyway."

She closes the distance between us and offers me her hand. I stow the trigger cord, take it, and pull her into a hug.

"I'm sorry," she says, and I can hear the tears in her voice.

"I know," I say. "It's okay, Cat. You did what you had to do."

We stand there for another ten seconds, until she finally says, "Hugging in armor is weird."

She's not wrong.

I let her go, and the three of us walk back to the dome together.

I'M BACK IN my rack, stretched out on the bed with my eyes closed and my hands folded behind my head, just thinking about drifting off, when Eight's death finally hits me. It makes no sense for so many reasons—I mean, even setting aside the fact that he pretty much had to go if I was going to stay, and also the fact that he was kind of annoying most of the time, and that I only actually knew him for a few days, he's not really gone, is he? After all, I'm him, and he was me. It's like mourning your reflection when you've broken a mirror.

Doesn't matter. Maybe it's for him, or maybe it's for me, or maybe it's just a release of everything that's been building up inside me ever since I fell down that fucking hole, but in the span of five seconds I go from totally fine to full-on ugly crying.

That goes on for a while.

I'm just winding down when someone knocks at my door.

"Come," I say, then sit up, swing my feet to the floor, and wipe my face mostly clean with the front of my shirt. When I look up, Nasha's closing the door behind her.

"Hey," she says softly. "Welcome back."

"Thanks." I shift to make room, and she sits down on the bed beside me. "Sorry it's just me this time."

She laughs, then slides an arm around my shoulder and rests the side of her head against mine. "Was it bad, what happened to Eight?"

I shrug. "I don't know. We were separated. He'd found a . . . nest, I guess? Thousands of creepers crawling over one another in a huge domed cavern. He was sending me stills of it when his signal cut." I can feel her shudder against me. "It must have been quick, anyway. He was set on pulling the trigger. Whatever happened to him, it was sudden enough that he didn't get the chance."

I don't really know that, of course. He was me, after all. Maybe he had a change of heart at the last minute. Maybe he could have pulled the trigger, but chose not to.

Nasha sniffles, then laughs.

"Sorry," she says. "I have no idea what to feel right now."

I slide my arm around her waist. She sighs, leans into me, and pushes me down onto the bed.

"You know," she says as she settles her head against my chest, "Marshall actually tried to order me to do a bombing run on your friends out there."

"Huh," I say, my eyes already drifting shut. "What did you say?"

She laughs again, softly, and slides one leg across mine. "I said that if what you told us is true, they're buried under a hundred or more meters of bedrock, and we don't have anything in our arsenal at this point that's powerful enough to so much as knock the dust off of their chandeliers. The most we could hope to do would be to annoy them, and that seems like a bad idea right now."

"Good call. How'd he take it?"

She slides her hand up my chest, cups my cheek, and pulls my head up far enough to kiss me. "About how you'd expect."

She settles in again, then reaches up to stroke my cheek. "Is it true?"

I kiss her hand, then move it back down to my chest. "Is what true?"

"What you told us," she says. "About the creepers. Are they really gonna leave us be?"

I shrug. "I think so? The truth is, though, that I don't know for sure how much either one of us understood what the other was saying. They said they'd leave us alone as long as we stayed clear of their tunnels and didn't try to build anything in the foot-hills south of the dome. Do they actually know what 'the dome' means, though? Are they totally clear on the fact that leaving us alone implies not grabbing the occasional human and tearing him to shreds? Who the hell knows?"

"Wow," she says. "You're a hell of a negotiator, huh?"

"Sorry," I say. "I did my best, you know?"

She rises up on one elbow, kisses my cheek, and then pulls my arm back around her and nuzzles her head into the hollow be-tween my shoulder and neck. "I know you did, babe." She sighs, and pulls me closer. "I know you did."

It's no more than a minute or two more before she's sleeping. I'm drifting as well. It's been a long few days. I close my eyes, and soon enough I slide into the dream of the caterpillar. We're back on Midgard, sitting across the backward-burning campfire from one another, watching the smoke spiral down out of a clear black sky.

"Is this an ending," he asks, "or a beginning?"

I look up from the fire. "You can speak now?"

"I could always speak. You couldn't understand."

I shrug. That's fair.

"I think it's both," I say. "I hope it's both."

That seems to satisfy him. We sit together then in companion-able silence until, bit by bit, he fades away.

Nasha's gone when I wake. She's left a message on my tablet, though.

Gotta fly today. See you when I'm back?

That makes me smile. I get out of bed, give myself a quick dry-scrub, and pull on my last set of semi-clean clothes.

I can't quite pin it down, but something is different today.

I feel a weird sense of . . . lightness? I don't know. I just . . .

And then it hits me. For the first time in I have no idea how long, *I'm not afraid.*

I'm savoring that feeling, wallowing in it, letting it soak straight into my bones, when my ocular pings.

<Command1>:You are required to report to the Commander's office immediately.

<Command1>:Failure to do so by 09:00 will be construed as desertion.

Oh well. So much for that.

I take my time responding to Marshall's summons. I've got

a pretty good idea what he's planning to say to me, and I don't want to hear it.

It's 08:59 when I open the door to Marshall's office. He's leaned back behind his desk, hands folded across his belly, with what could almost be a subtle half smile on his face.

Huh. That is not what I was expecting.

"Barnes," he says. "Have a seat."

I step into the office, close the door behind me, and pull a chair up to the desk.

"Good morning, sir. You asked to see me?"

"Yes," he says. "I did. Mostly, I wanted to apologize to you."

That's *really* not what I was expecting.

"It seems," he continues, "that I misjudged the situation yesterday. When I learned that you'd left our device with those creatures, when I learned that you'd told them what it was, well . . ."

"As I explained," I say, "I didn't leave the device with them. They seized it from Eight when they killed him. I had to explain what it was and how it operated, or they might have triggered it accidentally."

He nods. "You did mention that. I naturally assumed that they would immediately turn our weapon back on us. However, the fact that we're sitting here having this conversation tells me that I was wrong. I was wrong, and you were right. So, again—I apologize. I should not have reacted the way I did yesterday."

"You mean when you tried to get Cat and Lucas to kill me?"

His right eye twitches, but beyond that he maintains his composure. "Yes, Barnes. That was wrong. I'm sorry."

"Huh. Well. Apology accepted, I guess?"

"Excellent," he says. "You're a bigger man than most."

He leans forward, and reaches across the desk to offer me his hand. After a moment's hesitation, I shake it.

"So," I say when he releases me and leans back again. "Um . . . will that be all, sir?"

"Well," he says, and the smile returns, slightly bigger this time. "Not quite. Now that things are hopefully on their way back to normal, we have a job for you."

Right. Here we go. "A job, sir?"

"Yes," he says. "Assuming that our friends will keep to their tunnels and away from our dome in the future—and I hope we can assume that—it's time for us all to get back to the business of making sure this colony survives, don't you think?"

I lean back in my own chair and fold my arms across my chest. "Yes, sir. I suppose it is."

"Good. Good. Well, as I'm sure you can guess, producing those two devices yesterday put a dangerous dent in our remaining store of antimatter. We don't have any prospect of being able to produce new fuel stores anytime in the foreseeable future, and I'm sure I don't need to tell you what happens to all of us if our power plant shuts down."

"No," I say. "I'm sure you don't."

He leans forward now and plants both elbows on the desk, looking for all the world like a flitter salesman trying to close a deal.

"Half the fuel we pulled is lost, of course. No help for that. It is vital, however, that the antimatter contained in the device that you brought back with you goes back into the core."

Oh, for shit's sake.

"You pulled it out," I say. "Just do whatever you did then, only backward."

He tries for a sorrowful look now, but it's not working. "Unfortunately, that's not possible. We extracted that fuel by using the normal drive feed mechanism. As I'm sure you know, that only runs in one direction. There is no mechanism for feeding individual fuel elements back into the core. I'm afraid it's going to have to be done manually, from the inside."

I close my eyes, take a deep breath in, and let it out slowly.

What's the neutron flux in an active antimatter core? I don't think Jemma ever covered that one, but I'm guessing it's a lot.

"Don't worry," he says. "I won't ask you to upload before or after. You won't need to remember any of this."

"I won't have to upload?"

He shakes his head. "Absolutely not."

"I haven't uploaded since I came out of the tank, you know. If I do this, it'll be like this part of me never existed."

"Nonsense," he says. "This part of you, as you say, will have saved the colony. We'll remember, even if you don't." He looks down at his hands, then back up with what might even be sincere emotion. "I know I don't say this often enough, but the truth is, you've saved this colony more than once already, and I'm sure you will again in the future. That's a debt that can't be repaid. On behalf of all of us—thank you, Mickey. Your courage is an inspiration."

Mickey. For the first time in nine fucking years, he called me Mickey.

My courage is an inspiration.

Fuck you, Marshall.

I slide my chair back and get to my feet.

"No."

The sincerity drops from his face like a mask, replaced almost instantly by pure rage.

"What?"

"No," I say. "I won't do it. You obviously had plans for the colony to survive without that fuel when you sent me down into the tunnels. Use those. Or burn a drone getting your war-crime bomb back into the core. Or do it yourself. I'm not doing it."

He surges to his feet now, his face darkening and his eyes narrowing to slits.

"You will do it," he hisses. "You will, or as God is my witness I will wipe your pattern and your recordings from the servers, and I will shove the last instantiation of you down the corpse hole myself."

Now that the decision is made, I can feel a weight that I didn't realize was there lifting from my shoulders. It almost feels like flying.

"You can wipe the servers, Marshall. In fact, please do, because I am hereby resigning as this colony's Expendable. Find a replacement. I honestly don't care. You won't kill me, though, because I'm your only liaison to the creepers, and you were stupid enough to hand them an antimatter bomb yesterday. Have your people lay a hand on me, and I'll tell the creepers that the truce is off."

His mouth opens, closes, then opens again.

I can't help it. I burst out laughing.

"You wouldn't fucking dare," he finally manages when I'm halfway out the door.

"I've died seven goddamn times," I say over my shoulder. "That's six times more than anyone should. Don't tell me what I wouldn't dare."

I don't bother to close the door behind me.

"Hey, there, buddy. How's it going?"

I look up from my cricket and yam scramble. Berto sets his tray down on the table across from mine and drops onto the bench.

"Oh," I say. "It's you."

"Yeah," he says. "I heard you resigned."

I shrug. "Seems like it."

"Wild," he says. "I didn't know you could do that."

"You can't," I say. "Not unless you're holding an antimatter bomb over Marshall's head, anyway."

He takes a bite, chews, and swallows. I'm just turning back to my own food when he says, "Back on a solid diet, huh?"

"Yeah," I say. "I'm not sharing a ration anymore, am I?"

"Oh," he says. "Right."

"Yeah."

We eat in silence for a solid minute, long enough to be uncomfortable if I cared about that kind of stuff right now.

"I'm glad you made it back," he says finally.

I look up. "Thanks, I guess. Didn't feel up to inventing some story about what happened to me for Nine, huh?"

That gets a wince out of him, anyway. "Ouch. I said I was sorry about that."

"Yeah," I say. "You did."

We sit through another thirty seconds of silence. I'm almost done eating by now, but Berto's barely touched his food.

"So," he says. "Are we, uh . . . good?"

I close my eyes, take a deep breath in, and let it out. When I open them again, he's watching me expectantly. I lean across the table toward him. He leans forward in response.

I pop him right in the eye, hard enough to split my knuckle and snap his head back.

"Yeah," I say. "We're good."

I stand, pick up my tray, and go. When I glance back as the door to the corridor slides open, he's staring at me, mouth slightly open, hands flat on the table in front of him. The eye is already purpling up nicely.

I know it's a cliché, but I don't care. This is the first day of the rest of my life.

So apparently there's such a thing as springtime on Niflheim. Who knew?

About a year post-landfall, the temperature starts rising and the snow begins to melt. We get our first look at exposed soil a few weeks later. A month after that, the ground is covered in lichen.

Nobody seems to have a clear explanation for why this is happening. Niflheim's orbit is nearly circular, and its axial tilt is negligible. We shouldn't have seasons of any kind here, theoretically. The best guess that anyone can come up with about what's happening is that our sun is actually a marginally variable star, and its cycle is on the upswing.

That's the sort of thing you'd think the mission planners back on Midgard would have been aware of, isn't it? I mean, they observed this place for almost thirty years before we boosted out. After a little digging, I find out that they did observe a periodic swing in observed stellar output here. It was pretty well documented. They didn't ascribe it to the star, though, because nobody had a decent theory as to how that would work from a stellar physics standpoint. Instead, they decided that it must have had something to do with dust clouds in the interstellar medium, and then they filed it away. That's why they thought we'd be warm and happy here. They thought the high marks for stellar output were the real deal, and the low points were due to interference.

Oops.

At first everyone is pretty happy about the change in the weather, until some guy in the Physics Section thinks to wonder whether we're going to swing from one extreme to the other and wind up roasting in our own juices.

Spooky thought, but we don't. After a few months things level out somewhere between brisk and balmy, and eventually the folks in Agriculture actually manage to get an experimental plot going outside the dome.

It's right around that time, when our fellow colonists are finally starting to spend a bit of time outside and they're talking about decanting the first few embryos and everyone other than me and Marshall seems to have mostly forgotten about the creepers, that I ask Nasha if she'd like to go for a walk.

We still have to wear rebreathers. The partial pressure of oxygen has been rising, slowly but perceptibly, since green things started growing, but the change won't be enough to keep one of us alive unaided for a long while yet—if it ever is, of course. We have no idea how long this season will last. It could be years. It could be over tomorrow.

In the meantime, though, it's a nice day for a hike.

"Where are we going?" Nasha asks after Lucas has waved us through the perimeter.

"Away from the dome. Isn't that enough?"

She takes my hand, and we walk.

Back on Midgard, there was an enormous desert that straddled the equator and stretched nearly the width of the only continent.

Broad swaths of land there could go years without seeing any significant rain. Every once in a long while, though, when weather conditions were just right, a massive storm would roll over and dump a year's worth of water over those bone-dry plains and arroyos in a day or two. Whenever that happened, we got a reminder that life had been waiting there, poised to spring out at the first opportunity. Plants practically leapt out of the mud, and animals crawled up out of hibernation to eat and drink and hunt and mate.

Niflheim's biosphere seems to be a bit like that. The snow has only been gone for a couple of months, but already the lichen has given way to something that could be grass, and there are even a few woody-looking shrubs poking up here and there. There are animals too—mostly little crawly things that bear a striking resemblance to the creepers, but a klick or so out from the dome I spot what looks like an eight-legged reptile sunning itself on an exposed shelf of rock.

When I point it out to Nasha, she scowls and puts a hand to the burner she's brought along, because of course she did.

"Come on," I say. "It's cute."

She shoots me a sideways glance, then shakes her head and lets her hand fall to her side.

We keep walking.

After another five minutes or so, I have to stop to get my bearings. It's been a long time now, and everything looks so different without the snow. Nasha takes a half step back, folds her arms across her chest, and tilts her head to one side.

"This isn't just a walk-around, is it?"

I smile behind my rebreather. "Not exactly. I needed to check on something."

I've got my landmark now. We start up a hillside, then turn down into a gully that takes us out of sight of the dome.

"You sure about this?" Nasha asks. I glance back. Her hand is back on the burner. "This looks like creeper country."

"Yeah," I say. "We're actually pretty close to an entrance to their tunnel system."

"Okay," she says. "Why?"

"I told you," I say. "I have to check on something."

I miss the spot at first. The boulder I'd taken as my marker must have been held in place by the ice, or maybe it was pushed down the slope by runoff. In any case, it's twenty meters or more down the gully from where it was supposed to be. I finally recognize it, though, and once I've done that it's not too difficult to trace back to the little shelf where it was resting when I came out of the tunnels. Under that shelf is a jumble of smaller rocks. I drop to my knees and start pulling them away.

"Mickey?" Nasha says. "Do you want to tell me what we're doing here?"

I would, but I don't have to, because by now I've pulled enough of the scree out of the way to expose the hollow space under the rock shelf.

"Holy shit," Nasha says.

I turn back to look at her, to gauge her reaction. She's surprised, but not horrified or murderous. I take that as a good sign. Carefully, I reach into the dark space and pull Eight's pack out into the light.

"You sneaky little shit," she says.

I laugh. "You didn't think I'd actually leave this with the creepers, did you?"

She crouches down beside me, reaches out, and runs a hand across the top of the pack. "How?"

"How what? How did I manage to get this atrocity back from the creepers after they'd murdered Eight?"

Nasha turns to look at me. I can tell from her eyes that she's not smiling under the rebreather. "Yeah, Mickey."

I shrug. "I asked for it."

She shakes her head, then turns her attention back to the bomb. "Is it loaded?"

"Well, there's enough antimatter in here to sterilize a medium-sized city, if that's what you mean."

She pulls her hand back.

"Don't worry," I say. "As long as the bubbles are intact, the antimatter is basically in a different universe. It can't touch us."

"And what if some of them aren't intact?"

I laugh. "Trust me. You'd know."

"Why, Mickey?"

"Why, what? Why did I leave a doomsday weapon buried out here like pirate's treasure?"

"Yeah," she says. "That."

I rock back on my heels and turn to look at her. "Well, here's the thing. If I'd actually left it with the creepers like I told Marshall, they might have eventually gotten it into their heads to use it. I honestly couldn't have given a shit about most of the people in that dome at that point, but . . ."

She grins. "But what, Mickey?"

"You know," I say. "I'd rather let Marshall shove me down the corpse hole than risk having anything happen to you."

"Okay," she says. "I get that. So why didn't you bring it back?"

"Oh, that's easy. If I'd turned both bombs back over to Marshall, he definitely would have killed me on the spot, and then he would have sent Nine down into the tunnels to finish his genocide. The only reason I'm still alive, and the only reason the creepers are still here, is that he thinks I'm the only thing keeping the creepers from popping this thing off underneath the dome."

"I guess you're probably right about that," she says. "The part I don't get, though, is why the creepers let you walk out with both bombs. Weren't they worried about deterrence or whatever?"

I laugh again, a little harder. "Seriously? You think I actually told them what we were carrying? You think I told them we came into their home with the intent of committing genocide? Holy crow, Nasha. I'm no genius, but I'm not *that* dumb."

She seems taken aback by that. Apparently she thought I actually was that dumb.

"So what did you tell them?"

"I mean, the language thing was a major barrier, but I tried to tell them we were emissaries. They never actually asked about the packs. They don't really look like doomsday weapons, do they?"

"No," Nasha says. "I guess not."

I shove the pack back into the hollow, and then carefully push the rocks back into place until it's invisible again. When I'm done, I get to my feet and take a half dozen steps back to examine my work.

"What do you think?" I ask Nasha. "Will it stay hidden there?"

She shrugs. "Maybe for now. Probably not forever. Do you have a long-term plan, or are you just going to wait around until somebody stumbles across this place and accidentally kills us all?"

I sigh. "My plan was to wait until Marshall dies, then come back here and get it, and tell whoever the new commander is that the creepers decided to return the bomb as a gesture of goodwill."

"Seriously?"

"Yeah, seriously. If you've got a better plan, I'd love to hear it."

She stares back at me for a long moment, then shakes her head. "I've got nothing. How long do you expect this to go on, though? Is Marshall sick?"

"Not that I know of."

She takes my hand. "Do you have a backup plan, just in case he doesn't die?"

"I do not."

She cups my cheek in her free hand, then lifts her rebreather and leans in to kiss me. "You really aren't a genius," she says, then lets my hand fall and turns to start back up the gully. "It's a good thing you're cute."

I turn to look back at the bomb's hiding place. It just looks like a jumble of rocks, no different from all the other jumbles of rocks that cover ninety percent of this planet.

Is it good enough?

Marshall seems pretty healthy.

I guess it'll have to be.

With a final backward glance, I put our would-be war crime behind me.

I follow Nasha out of the shadows, up the gully, and into the sun.

Acknowledgments

The list of people who contributed to this book is a long one. I'm probably going to forget some of them. If you're one of those, I hope you will forgive me. As you are probably well aware, I'm not nearly as smart as I look.

First, the obvious: my deepest gratitude to Paul Lucas and the good folks at Janklow & Nesbit, without whose guidance and encouragement I would almost certainly have given up on this business long ago, and also to Michael Rowley of Rebellion Publishing and Michael Homler of St. Martin's Press, both of whom were willing to take a chance on an odd little book written by an extremely obscure author. Slightly less obviously, I would also like to give sincere and heartfelt thanks to Navah Wolfe, who read this story when it was a modestly depressing novella and encouraged me to turn it into a much less depressing novel. If you read this, Navah, I hope you see your fingerprints on the final product, and I do hope that you approve.

My sincere thanks also go out to (in no particular order):

- Kira and Claire, for their tough but fair criticism of the earliest drafts of this story.
- Heather, for buying me endless chais on my own credit card.
- Anthony Taboni, for being the future president of my nascent fan club.
- Therese, Craig, Kim, Aaron, and Gary, for reading through multiple versions of this manuscript without ever telling me to just pack it in already.
- Karen Fish, for teaching me what it means to be a writer.
- John, for being my go-to sounding board on all things literary.
- Mickey, for not getting mad after I put him into a book and then murdered him multiple times.
- Jack, for keeping my ego in check when it was needed most.
- Jen, for finally reading one of my manuscripts prepublication.
- Max and Freya, for never letting me forget what's really important in life.

As I said, this is a partial list. This book would not be what it is without any of these folks, and probably a whole mess of others besides. Thanks, friends. Now on to the next one, right?

Turn the page for a sneak peek at
Edward Ashton's new novel

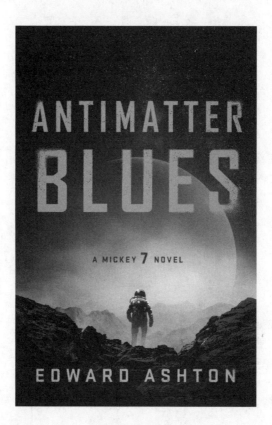

Available Early 2023

Copyright © 2023 by Edward Ashton

001

"I JUST SAW myself in the corridor."

Nasha looks up from her tablet. She's sitting in our desk chair, feet propped up on our bed, wearing nothing but underwear and boots. That's not a look that many people can pull off, but Nasha manages it with aplomb. She pushes her braids back from her face and drops her feet to the floor.

"Nice to see you too," she says. "Close the door."

I step into the room and let the door latch behind me. My rack looks a lot smaller than it did before Nasha moved in. The first thing she did when she got here was shove her bed in beside mine to make an almost-double, and the second was to fill up most of the remaining floor space with a meter-long footlocker that I'm not allowed to go into. Also, for some reason Nasha herself takes up a lot more space than her actual size would lead you to believe.

To be clear: I am not complaining about any of this.

I sit down on the bed and take the tablet from her hands. A look of annoyance flashes across her face, but she doesn't resist.

"Did you hear me? *I saw another me.* He was on the bottom

level, near the cycler. I think Marshall has started pulling new copies of me out of the tank."

Nasha sighs. "That's impossible, Mickey. Marshall wiped your patterns when you resigned, right?"

"Yeah," I say. "I mean, I think so. He said he was going to."

"And he hasn't pulled anyone out of the tank in the meantime, right?"

"I don't think so. Berto told me they wound up burning two drones when they shoved the fuel from my bubble bomb back into the reactor. I doubt they would have wasted those kinds of resources if they'd had a bunch of extra Mickeys lying around."

She leans back and props her feet up on the bed beside me. "Right. So unless Eight's really been hanging out with the creepers for the last two years and just decided to rejoin us, you couldn't have seen yourself wandering around the corridors. Are you sure it wasn't Harrison?"

"Harrison? You mean Jamie Harrison?"

She grins. "Yeah. He's like your doppelgänger, right? I could definitely see you mistaking him for you."

Jamie Harrison works in Agriculture. He takes care of the rabbits, mostly. He's short and skinny, with mousy brown hair that sticks up from his head in tufts, a perpetual nervous squint, and a prominent overbite. He looks *nothing* like me.

I don't think he looks anything like me, anyway.

"Look," I say. "I know what I saw, and what I saw was me. Maggie Ling was hustling him down Spoke Three toward the hub. They crossed in front of me just past Medical. They were probably twenty meters away and I only saw them for a second, but I know what I look like. It was definitely me."

Nasha's grin fades. "The hub, huh? And he was with Maggie?"

Maggie Ling is head of Systems Engineering. The last couple of times she hustled me somewhere, I wound up dying of radiation poisoning within the hour.

"You believe me now?"

She shakes her head. "Didn't say that. Let's assume you're right, though. After two years, however he managed it and for whatever reason, Marshall decided to pull Mickey9 out of the tank. What would he be doing with Maggie Ling, on the bottom level, headed toward the hub?"

I can feel my face twisting into a scowl. "The reactor."

"Yeah," she says. "That seems like the most likely bet, doesn't it?"

Mucking around inside the antimatter reactor is a prime job for an Expendable. We can withstand the neutron flux in there for longer than a drone can, and when we die, we're a hell of a lot easier to replace. Just chuck the old body in the cycler, fire up the bio-printer, and wait a few hours.

Of course, I'm not an Expendable anymore. I'm retired.

Unless I'm not, I guess.

"Anyway," Nasha says, "whatever's going on, it's not really your problem, is it?"

I've got a lot to say to that. What's my obligation to care about what happens to another instantiation of me? Is that *me* getting irradiated, or is it just some other guy who looks like me? What does the Ship of Theseus have to say about a damaged hull that gets left behind on an island somewhere and forgotten? But after five seconds of opening my mouth, changing my mind, and then closing it again, all I manage to come out with is, "What?"

"Think about it," Nasha says. "What's the worst-case scenario here?"

"Um . . . that Maggie Ling just sent a copy of me into the reactor core?"

"Right. So something needed to get done, and she did it. If she hadn't pulled a *new* Mickey out of the tank to do it, what would her alternative have been?"

I know the answer to this one. Nasha stands, then pulls me to my feet and into a kiss.

"Worst case," she says, "is that somebody just got sent into the core, *and that somebody wasn't you.* I don't know about you, babe, but you know what? I'll take it."

So here's a solid fact: Warm Niflheim is a much nicer place than Cold Niflheim. It's green and wet and covered with all manner of crawly things. You can even go outside now without wrapping yourself up in six layers of thermals. You'll still need a rebreather, but the partial pressure of oxygen is almost twenty percent higher now than it was when we made landfall, so you won't feel quite so much like you're drowning while you're walking around. On a good day, you can almost imagine that we've found the sort of place that they promised us when we boarded the *Drakkar*.

Here's another solid fact: Warm Niflheim isn't going to last forever. Winter is coming.

Miko Berrigan and his minions in Physics have spent most of the summer poring over records of the thirty years of observations that were made of Niflheim's sun before the *Drakkar* boosted out. There were three warm spells in that period. The longest lasted seven years. The shortest was eleven months. The four winters that surrounded them ranged from two years to nine. The transitions weren't abrupt, and they weren't smooth. They were marked by lengthening oscillations between hot and cold that eventually stabilized into one steady state or the other. The season we're in now went through a half dozen false starts before it really settled in.

The physicists back on Midgard thought what they were seeing was all due to interference from interstellar dust. Cute, right?

We haven't been wasting the summer. Hieronymus Marshall is a jackass, but he isn't stupid, and he wants this colony to live. We've been stockpiling food, studying the local fauna to figure out how they survive the winters, building out the dome to accommodate the first round of decanted embryos, releasing engineered algae that are supposed to begin the work of pushing the atmosphere further toward something we can breathe, etc., etc., etc.

The problem is that it all takes time, and that's something we don't have an infinite supply of. All the things that keep us alive here take enormous amounts of power, and right now the only real power source we have is the *Drakkar*'s antimatter reactor, still spinning away under the hub, slowly drawing down the last of the fuel supply that brought us here.

Which brings me back to Maggie Ling, hustling another me down Spoke Three toward the hub. Without the reactor, we might just barely be able to get by, as long as the weather holds.

That's the thing, though. The weather is not going to hold.

I'VE SPENT ALMOST all of my work shifts since my resignation with Agriculture. This isn't because I have a green thumb or anything. It's mostly by default. I don't have the qualifications to do anything useful for Physics or Biology or Engineering. Amundsen in Security is tight with Marshall and also is still down on me for losing consciousness while Cat and I were fighting creepers on the perimeter two years ago, so he mostly wants nothing to do with me these days. I'll probably get to spend some time changing diapers in the crèche once they start pulling babies out of cold storage, but that's still on hold at the moment, pending a bit more confidence that we can keep them alive once they're decanted.

So, that leaves me with Agriculture. On this day, in fact, I'm hanging with Jamie Harrison, taking care of the rabbits.

You might be wondering why we keep rabbits in a closed-loop ecological system. Raising animals for meat can be a net source of calories in a place where they can more or less fend for themselves, staying alive by eating things like grass and weeds that we wouldn't or couldn't eat. On Niflheim, though, that kind of thing is still entirely aspirational. Rabbits can't eat the lichen and ferns that surround the dome now. The proteins that the natives use here are folded the wrong way for Union life. Instead we feed them tomato vines and potato greens and protein slurry, some of which gets converted into edible rabbit parts but most of which just gets burned up by their stupid mammalian metabolisms or turned into poop. At the end of the day, every kcal of edible rabbit meat costs us about three kcal of other stuff that we could conceivably have just eaten ourselves, as well as a huge pile of stuff that we can't eat, but that could have gone back into the cycler. Rabbits are a massive luxury item in a place that is notably short on pretty much any other type of luxury. So, why do we do it?

Well, for one, rabbits are cute. Numerous psychological studies over the past thousand years of the diaspora have shown that humans need a certain amount of cuddliness in their lives, and rabbits are the only things on Niflheim that provide that for us.

Of course, they're also delicious. As soon as they reach full growth, it's off to the kitchen with these guys. In the meantime, though, they're a lot more fun to hang around with than most of the people in this colony.

Jamie, on the other hand, is neither cute nor fun to hang around with.

Rabbits on Niflheim are treated essentially the same way maximum-security prisoners were treated back on Midgard.

They spend the vast majority of their time crammed into three small hutches pushed up against a wall next to the hydroponics tanks. Once a day, we let them out one hutch at a time into a slightly larger space bounded by a bulkhead on two sides and a short white wire fence on the other. They hop around a little, get whatever exercise they can, hang out with anyone who (a) needs a cuteness fix and (b) has sterilized themselves to Jamie's satisfaction, and then get plopped back into the hutch for another day, where they while away the time eating, pooping, and making more rabbits.

It's not a terrible life.

It's better than mine in a lot of ways, if I'm being honest.

If I had any choice about my duty cycles, I'd probably spend most of them here. I don't, though. I get to hang with the rabbits during working hours when Jamie puts in a request for my services, and that only happens on two occasions. One is culling day, which is when I get to go through the hutches and pick out the males who are big enough for eating and the females who are old enough that their reproduction has started to slow down. The other, like today, is hutch-cleaning day.

The good thing about hutch-cleaning day is that Jamie doesn't trust me to do it properly. That means I get to spend the day wrangling the rabbits while he does most of the actual work.

I've just finished pulling the last of the kits out of Hutch One and dropping them off in the exercise yard when the door to the corridor slides open and Berto steps through.

Great.

"Hey," he says. "How's my dinner doing?"

I sigh, straighten, and turn to face him. He steps over the fence and crouches down to stroke a kit's ears with one finger.

"Hands off, Gomez," Jamie says without turning away from whatever he's doing in the hutch. "You're not sterile."

Berto laughs. "Sterile? These things are rats in fancy suits, Jamie. You're literally scooping piles of shit out of their house right now. If anyone should be worried about contamination, it's me."

"This is not a debate," Jamie says. "Get your hands off of my animals or get out of my space. I can have Security down here in less than a minute."

Berto's smile disappears, and it looks like he's going to argue. In the end, though, he shakes his head and stands.

"Jamie's right," I say. "You know that, don't you? These poor guys spend nine-tenths of their time crawling all over each other in the hutches. If you get one of them sick, they'll all be dead in a week, and it's not like we have a backup supply around here anywhere."

"Whatever," Berto says. "I didn't come down here to play with the bunnies."

I wait for him to go on. After a long five seconds, I raise one eyebrow and say, "So . . ."

His expression shifts from annoyed to confused. "So, what?"

I roll my eyes. "Why *did* you come down here, Berto?"

He grins. "Oh. I was bored, mostly. Didn't Nasha tell you?"

Now it's my turn to be confused. "Tell me what?"

"We're grounded," he says. "No more aerial reconnaissance until further notice."

Huh.

"No," I say. "Nasha didn't mention that. When did this happen?"

"I found out this morning when I showed up for my shift. Maybe they haven't told her yet?"

"Yeah. Maybe. Did they tell you why?"

He shakes his head. "Not really. The tech on duty said something about not being able to charge the gravitic grids, but that doesn't make any sense. We've got an antimatter reactor, right? It's not like we need to ration power."

"Yeah," I say. "You wouldn't think so."

"Not like it matters. I'm pretty confident at this point that there's nothing out there that's a threat to us other than the creepers, and I haven't seen one of them within five klicks of the dome since the weather turned. Don't get me wrong. I'd rather be flying than . . . well, than pretty much anything, I guess. I'm not kidding myself, though. Aerial reconnaissance at this point is a waste of time and resources."

One of the rabbits is nosing at my boot. I crouch down to give his ears a scratch. "So if, just hypothetically speaking, we did have some kind of issue with power generation, grounding you and Nasha might be a good place to cut back, huh?"

He shrugs. "I guess so. Gravitic grids are power hogs. Those lifters use an ungodly amount of juice." He hesitates, and his grin fades. "Do you know something, Mickey?"

The rabbit nips at my finger. I guess he wasn't looking for affection after all. I nudge him away with one hand, then stand again and glance back at Jamie. He's head and shoulders deep in the hutch, scrubbing at something with a disinfectant sponge.

"Look," I say, "have you seen me around recently?"

His mouth opens, then closes again. He shakes his head. "What?"

"Have you seen me?" I say. "Maybe with someone from Engineering? Maybe looking kind of confused?"

His eyes narrow. "What are you saying, Mickey?"

I sigh. "I'm saying I think I saw another me this morning. I think Marshall is pulling Mickeys out of the tank again."

He tilts his head to one side and folds his arms across his chest. "You're saying that you think Hieronymus Marshall, Niflheim's high priest of Natalism, is deliberately creating multiples?"

I hesitate, then shake my head. "It sounds stupid when you say it like that."

"Yeah," he says. "That's because it *is* stupid. Did you actually see another Mickey somewhere? Did you talk to him?"

"I didn't talk to him, but I saw him. For a second. From about twenty meters away."

Berto rolls his eyes. "So you got a glance of someone from twenty meters off that kind of looked like you, and from that you've concluded that our commander, who has a visceral, religiously motivated hatred of multiples in general, and of you in particular, is secretly making more of you because . . ."

"Look," I say, "I know what I saw."

"You don't," he says, and gestures toward the hutch. "It was probably just Jamie. You two are like twins."

Et tu, Berto?

I open my mouth to argue, or maybe to tell him to go fuck himself, but before I can decide which one he smacks me on the shoulder and says, "Anyway, it doesn't matter, does it? What do you care if Marshall is pulling copies of you out of the tank and . . . I don't know . . . making them fight to the death while he and Amundsen take bets on the winner? You're retired, remember? How is this any skin off of your nose?"

That's a good question, actually. I've given it some thought since Nasha asked me the same basic question. If there's one thing I'm sure of after what happened with Eight two years ago, it's that I'm the only me there's ever going to be, no matter what Nine or Ten or whatever number they've gotten to by now might think about it. By that logic, if Marshall is pulling bodies out of the tank and throwing them into the reactor or making them play gladiator or whatever, it doesn't actually have anything to do with me, but . . .

But still.

It kind of does.

"Look," I say. "Forget about the whole morality thing. The person I thought was me was with Maggie Ling, and they were headed toward the reactor."

Berto starts to reply, but then his smile fades and I can see the wheels turning.

"Oh," he says finally.

"Yeah. And you just got grounded."

"Right," he says. "That might be a problem."

"You think? How long would we last here without power?"

"Depends," he says. "Are we without power because the reactor shut down gracefully and got decommissioned like it's eventually supposed to, or are we without power because the reactor overloaded and vaporized everything in a fifty-klick radius?"

"Let's assume option one."

He scratches the back of his head. "We'd probably be okay for the moment. We're still getting a fair amount of our calories from the cycler, I think, but that's something we can work on if we start throwing bodies at Agriculture. There's not much else going on around here that requires a ton of power and is also absolutely essential for our survival."

"That's for now. What about when the cold comes back?"

"Oh," Berto says. "When that happens we're totally fucked."

"Yeah," I say. "That's pretty much where I wound up."

He grimaces. "Okay. So what do we do?"

"I'm not sure we do anything. We've still got power at the moment and we haven't been vaporized, so obviously the reactor is still functioning. I guess default is to hope that Maggie knows what she's doing and that whatever's going on is just a temporary glitch."

Berto grimaces. "I've got plenty of confidence in Maggie, but if somebody's screwing around with the insides of the reactor, it's not her, is it?"

"Now, wait a minute," I say. "I hope you're not questioning *my* competence. If there's one thing I've proved I'm good at around here, it's fixing crap while picking up fatal doses of radiation."

"Yeah," Berto says. "That's a fair point. Still, I've got to say— just the thought of something glitching in the reactor is enough to spook me. Any thoughts on how we can figure out what the hell's going on?"

"Don't mean to interrupt," Jamie says from behind me, "but I'm finished here. If you hens are done clucking, would you mind getting these guys back into One so we can get started on Two?"

I look back at him. He scowls and points to the hutch.

"Sorry," I say to Berto. "Duty calls."

"Yeah," he says. "You do your bunny thing. I think I'm gonna do a little poking around. Ping me when you're off-shift, huh?"

"Sometime today," Jamie says.

Berto shoots him a glare, then steps back over the fence and goes.

WE'RE JUST GETTING the last of the rabbits back into Hutch Three when Jamie says, "You know, I heard what you and Gomez were saying earlier."

I turn to look at him. "Really? So what do you think?"

He shrugs. "I think Gomez can go screw. You don't look anything like me."

I open my mouth to reply, then shut it again as my brain processes what he just said.

"I'm not saying I'm *better*-looking than you," he says. "We're just different."

"So," I finally manage. "Out of all the stuff Berto and I were talking about, *that's* what you fixated on?"

"Yeah," he says. "Pretty much. Why? Was there something else that I ought to give a shit about?"

I know the screening process to get involved with this mission back on Midgard was incredibly rigorous. I know they only selected the best and the brightest. Jamie, though . . .

Maybe he was somebody's nephew?

I'm about to say something along the lines of, *Yes, I agree that we look nothing alike*, when my ocular pings.

> <Command1>: You are required to report to the Commander's office immediately.
>
> <Command1>: Failure to do so by 17:30 will be construed as insubordination.

Okay, then. Here we go.

JustTeeJay (JustTeeJay.com)

EDWARD ASHTON is the author of the novels *Three Days in April* and *The End of Ordinary,* as well as of short stories that have appeared in venues ranging from the newsletter of an Italian sausage company to *Escape Pod, Analog Science Fiction and Fact,* and *Fireside Magazine.* He lives in upstate New York in a cabin in the woods (not *that* cabin in the woods) with his wife, a variable number of daughters, and an adorably mopey dog named Max. In his free time, he enjoys cancer research, teaching quantum physics to sullen graduate students, and whittling. You can find him on Twitter @edashtonwriting and visit his website at edwardashton.com.